THE RISING MINDSET

16 Masterstrokes To Elevate Your Life

A Beginner's Guide to Mindset, Health, Finances, Relationships, Habits, Spirituality, Gratitude, Contributions and Much More...

Dr. Ravi Surana

INDIA · SINGAPORE · MALAYSIA

ISBN
Paperback 979-8-89556-033-4
Hardcase 979-8-89610-758-3

DISCLAIMER

This non fictional book incorporate fictional scenarios, including real –world places, companies, health care organisations and brands, to enhance engagement and reliability. These fictional elements are not meant to be taken as factual representations.

All brands, companies, organisations and locations mentioned in the book are owned by their respective owners. The author does not represent or endorse any entity referenced herein.

The characters Raghav, Baba, Vishwanath, Rajendra, Robin, Divina, Arnav, Dr Prisha, Yuvam, Aman and all others related conversations are entirely fictional. Any resemblance to actual individuals, living or deceased, or real events is coincidental.

The dialogues, characters, and situations presented in the book are products of the author's imagination. They are not intended to depict actual events or individuals.

The author disclaims any liability arising from actions taken based on information in this book

In the loving memory of my mother,
who departed just as this book was nearing completion;
I only wish she could have held this book in her hands.

Our greatest glory is not in never falling,
but in RISING every time we fall.

– Confucius

CONTENTS

PREFACE

This book first came into being on a rainy evening in Udaipur, India, in June 2022 when I sat down in a restaurant and enjoyed the lovely weather.

I welcome you to this journey of transformation! I would like to thank you for picking up this book. I hope the ideas given in this book will help you as much as they have helped me. I wanted that even school-going children can benefit from this book, that's why I kept the language of the book very simple.

The whole book is like a podcast between Baba and his grandson Raghav. Raghav wants to abstract all the moral values and life principles from his Baba. Baba is supposed to have a sound philosophy of life. His daily routine will help every reader to make his own daily routine. This book laid more emphasis on physical exercise, mindset, sound sleep, and better relationships.

I have immersed myself in the works of all-time great motivational speakers and authors like Brian Tracy, Zig Ziglar, Tony Robbins, Jack Canfield, James Clear, David Schwartz, Dale Carnegie, Napoleon Hill, Chetan Bhagat, and many others. I have read more than fifty books on personal efficiency and effectiveness in last one decade and have always believed in trying to make a difference in the lives of others by helping them to redefine their thinking. This book is the result of that.

As I started writing this book, each time I came across a good idea, I noted it down in my notepad. I wanted others to benefit from that idea.

This book will surely change your thought process in a positive manner and will teach you many moral values to lead a successful life. Some of the content of the book is so fresh and original that you won't find it in any other book in the world. Every idea in this book is focused on increasing your overall levels of productivity, performance, and output. You can apply many of these ideas in your personal life. This book will motivate you to travel more and learn by travelling across the globe.

Sometimes you may feel life's not going your way, and you also feel frustrated. You need some direction, and then it's a sign that your life needs balance. Just as a car balances on 4 wheels, we must balance 4 areas of life: our health, our relationships, our work life, and our social life. The content of this book is short so that you can read it repeatedly. Changing your thoughts doesn't happen overnight. Give yourself enough time to practice what you will read in this book. If you find this valuable, keep reading it again and again because we are forgetful beings.

This book is not just a collection of words; it's a catalyst for change. It's a reminder that you have the strength to overcome any obstacle, the courage to pursue your dreams, and the wisdom to create the life you desire. In the following pages, we will explore the depths of human resilience, the power of mindset, and the unwavering belief in oneself. We will delve into the stories of those who have faced adversity and emerged stronger, and uncover the secrets to their success. I wish you all the best on this journey with me. I hope you will enjoy every minute of it.

1

THE JOURNEY STARTS HERE

*"One day, your life will flash before your eyes.
Make sure it's worth watching."*

– Gerald way

It was 8:00 pm in Dubai with short downpours, the lights shone brightly on the grand stage, casting a warm glow over the packed auditorium. The air was electric with anticipation as the guests eagerly awaited the start of the prestigious award ceremony. The room was damn packed with who's who of the whole artificial intelligence-based information technology industry. The stage was set with a sleek, modern backdrop, adorned with the ceremony's logo and sponsors' names. A podium stood centre stage, flanked by one gleaming trophy display. The orchestra pit was filled with musicians. The energy in the room was palpable, with excitement building as the night wore on. As the lights dimmed slightly, a hush fell over the crowd. A charismatic figure took the stage, welcoming everyone to the ceremony. The audience applauded politely, and the show began.

The UAE AI and Robotics awards ceremony for good aims to encourage research and applications of innovative solutions in artificial intelligence and robotics to meet existing challenges in the categories of health, education, and social services are getting held. Throughout the evening, winners were announced, and the I. T recipients made their way one by one to accept their awards for creating the best robotic software programmes. There was applause, cheers, and occasional tears of joy.

As the final and the most awaited award of the day come, the trophy was presented. The name announced was Mr Raghav Das Maruti from India for his valuable contribution to the best artificial intelligence-based software development programme. The audience erupted into a standing ovation, congratulating the well-deserving winner. Raghav was requested to speak a few words behind his success story.

With mike in hand, Raghav started, "My dear ladies and gentlemen, esteemed guests, and all I.T. community members, today we have gathered here to welcome artificial intelligence in the field of I.T. It is my great honour to stand in front of you all today. Today is the birth anniversary of my late grandfather, Mr. Vishwanath. I called him Baba. He left us 2 years back, but I am reminded of him each and every day. Without his support, I would not have been here in front of you all today. He taught me 16 principles of life when I was just an ordinary frustrated new guy, just entered the I.T. industry. Today I want to talk about those 16 principles that matter deeply to me.

Today, I invite you to join me on a sentimental journey through time, back to a pivotal moment 3 years ago. It was a trip that changed my life when I travelled from Dubai to Jodhpur to visit my beloved grandfather, who is now etched forever in my memories."

Three Years Ago

"Raghav, this is Dr. Robin from Chandrakala Hospital in Jodhpur. I am calling to inform you that your grandpa is admitted to our hospital this morning. Unfortunately, he is suffering from pneumonia." Raghav's heart sank as he processed the news. He felt a wave of concern wash over him, mixed with memories of his beloved grandpa. He hadn't seen him in years, but the image of his vibrant personality remained etched in his mind.

"Robin, how is he? What happened?"

Raghav asked, trying to compose himself.

"I know your grandpa is living alone here," Robin continued, "but I had the pleasure of meeting him today. Despite his current condition, he still exudes the same liveliness, charm, and warmth that he held 12 years ago. His tall, fit stature and infectious jovial nature haven't changed a bit. He's still the same charismatic person. He is indeed a spry and vibrant 75-year-old, with a twinkle in his eye and a heart of gold. He exudes a sense of quiet confidence and authority, earned from a lifetime of wisdom, compassion, and integrity. He has a sharp mind and quick wit. He also remembers my pet name, Robo, which no one knows in this hospital. I have been working in this hospital as a junior resident for the last 2 years."

Raghav's eyes welled up with tears as he listened to Robin's words.

Is he really out of danger?" asked Raghav.

Nothing to worry about, but I still thought it's better to inform you.

How come he has become an encyclopaedia with so much knowledge and understanding of more than 10 languages? With the Gujarati receptionist, he was speaking in Gujarati; with the Kerala nurse, he was chatting in Malayalam; with the senior doctor from Hyderabad, he was cracking jokes in Telugu, and with me, he was speaking in English. At the age of 75, I was astonished to see his mind power and physical fitness. I have seen very few such lively patients in our hospital.

Sir, please come. There is an emergency case of heavy bleeding from the head; a drunken man has been hit by a taxi. Ok, bye Raghav. I will call you back later at night. Let me know if you are making any plans to see your grandpa by coming all the way from Dubai.

Memories of their time together flooded Raghav's mind, and he couldn't wait to see him. "Thank you for letting me knows, Robin, my friend. I'll be there as soon as possible," Raghav said, already planning his trip.

With tears in my eyes and proud of my grandpa, I have now decided to book my flight to Jodhpur as early as possible. I am so sorry, Divina, I won't be available this time to celebrate our wedding anniversary the day after tomorrow. Please search for the flight from Dubai to Jodhpur. I will prefer a direct flight, and this time I will spend a lot of time with Baba. I'm going to see him after 3 long years. He is the only elder left in my family after the death of my Maa and Paa. It's because of him that I did my schooling and higher studies. Without his support in childhood, I couldn't have grown up. He has a big heart. His character is built on a foundation of resilience, gratitude, and generosity. He is a true patriarch, with a legacy of love, laughter, and inspiration that spans generations. In his presence, you can't help but feel uplifted, motivated, and grateful for the encounter. He is no less than a gem, Divina. After the sudden demise of my Maa, Paa, and Dadi in a car accident 12 years ago, he had a very bad phase in his life. He was on vacation with his friends when he heard the news of the car accident. He reached home the next day. He cried a lot and was totally broken inside, but somehow he managed to come out of his worst time in a few months.

He was a true nature lover. Every day in the morning, he had a habit of going to the park to spend some leisure time with his friends. He had the ability to talk and make conversation with any stranger. He was also fond of cooking; every day, he spent some time in the kitchen trying new recipes. He was a great fan of Mr.Rajesh Khanna, one of the most successful actor in the history of Indian cinema. He watched his movie "Anand" many times and was very much inspired by his role. He always used to tell me, *"Zindagi lambi nahi, badi honi chahiye." (Life should not be long, it should be large.)*

The next month after my parent's death, he went to Rishikesh and spent a whole month there. He came back with a new enthusiasm, vibrant face, and more positivity. He always used to say that if you want to have a millionaire mind, travel more and more. He always lays emphasis on physical fitness. Every time he goes to the garden, he does some push-ups, plays cricket with small children, and never neglects his friends, always caring for poor people. He was determined to do things in his own ways. With time, he became enormously successful with a brilliant sense of humour.

So, Divina, as there is no direct flight from Dubai to Jodhpur, the plane will layover in Ahmadabad for 3 hours. Should I book this? Raghav, please book 2 tickets, I will also come with you.

No, Divina, I don't know how much time I would have to live in Jodhpur, and Yuvam has his half-yearly exams next month. So, I would advise you to take care of his studies. Last time, he topped his class in 4th standard. I want the same result in 5th standard. After all, you are a premier coach for him, especially in science and maths.

Raghav, we both will miss you so much. Please try to take Baba also with you to Dubai; we all will live together now. Yeah, Divina, I will try my best to convince him to come back with me, but I doubt he won't agree. So Divina, its 11 pm now. I have to reach the airport at 8.00 am. Please give me a tight hug, make my bed, and put off the lights. I need to wake up at 6.00 am in the morning.

The whole night, I couldn't sleep. Baba's memories were captivating me throughout the night like a laser beam.

The flight landed at Jodhpur Airport at 6 p.m. in the evening. It was an awesome experience to reach my country, India, after around 3 long years. I felt a bit relaxed but a little bit tired after a long flight. I booked a cab from the airport and reached directly to Chandrakala Hospital to see my Baba. Tears streamed down my face as I rode in the cab, my emotions overwhelming me. The driver, noticing my distress, asked gently, 'What's wrong?' I took a deep breath and explained, "I'm finally going to see my grandfather in the hospital after what feels like an eternity. The wait is almost over."

I dial Robin, "Hey friend, where are you? I have reached Jodhpur and now I'm in the cab going to the hospital." Robin told me, "Oh Raghav, I didn't believe you could reach Jodhpur within a day." "Wow, just come to ward no. 9, I am having tea with your Baba. He is giving me some knowledge about family and relations." "Oh Robin, order one coffee for me also. I will reach in 5 minutes." "Sure, Raghav."

The cab arrived at the hospital.

"Sir, who is admitted to this hospital," asked the cab driver.

And I replied, "My grandfather, but he is indeed my godfather."

Madam, where is ward no. 9? Sir, you have to take the lift from the right and go to the first floor. Thank you, madam.

Oh Baba, how did everything happen? I was not crying but so excited to meet him, the same charm on his face and fit and fine personality as he was 3 years ago. His eyes sparkle with kindness, and his gentle voice is laced with warmth and empathy. His presence is calming yet energising, like a soothing cup of tea on a chilly day. He has a gift for connecting with people from all walks of life, and his genuine interest in others is contagious. I touched his feet and hugged him tightly. Oh Robin, good to know that you have become a doc; you were a fantastic football player in school. Yes, Raghav, you do remember. Wow. I hugged Robin and thanked him for his help.

The senior doctor said that since all the tests are normal, we can discharge Baba tomorrow morning. Oh, that's great news. I will spend more time with Baba at home, thanks to the almighty. Robin and I had dinner together in the hospital canteen. The food was a bit less salty, but I was hungry so I didn't mind. I slept on the sofa in Baba's room, got up early in the morning, and went outside the hospital for tea. Later, I was busy packing Baba's bag, completing all the formalities and paperwork for discharge. All the hospital staff came one by one to meet Baba. Some brought flowers, some brought garlands. I was wondering what kind of aura he had created in the hospital. The scene was like someone retiring from his post. Many doctors and nursing staff took Baba's contact number and noted his address.

Now it was time to leave the hospital. Many doctors and hospital staff came out of the hospital with us. The ambulance arrived on time at noon, and Baba and I left the hospital.

After arriving home, I saw all the neighbours were waiting outside the house to greet Baba. Some were of his age group, others were of my age group, and some were children with whom Baba used to play cricket. I somehow managed to take Baba inside the house from the ambulance and greeted them patiently. I ordered tea from a nearby tea stall. The guests showed how much love and respect they had for Baba. Then, after 2 hours, we had dinner when the guests left. I got a video call from Divina; she was glad to see him coming home from the hospital in a short span of time. She advised me to take care of Baba for a week before he returns to his normal life. I decided to take a leave of around 10 days. During those 10 days, I will absorb more and more knowledge about baba's philosophy about life, relations, travel, nature, and success.

From the next morning itself, I started asking questions to Baba so that in these 10 days, I can get various solutions to various questions of life. The following are the list of questions I asked Baba, and answers were his timeless experiments and experiences of life.

2

GRATITUDE ENRICHES LIFE

"Acknowledging the good that you already have in your life is the foundation for all abundance."

– Eckhart Tolle

Baba, I have never seen you anxious, but in the real world, I have seen people so anxious. I myself sometimes feel low. Is there any method to recharge the battery of the mind? Do you have any sort of charger?

Well, Raghav, ups and downs, highs and lows are part of everyone's life. An ECG machine showing a straight line suggests a person is not alive. So, it's normal to be sad sometimes.

I suggest a very old technique given to me by Guru Govind Das. The technique is named "Count Your Blessings."

Whenever you feel low, just take out all the positive things you hold.

If you have a roof over your head, it's a blessing, which many don't have.

If you get your meals on time and clean water to drink, it's a blessing.

If you are fit to run, your hands are working, eyes to see the waves at shore, and ears to listen to drops of rain, feel yourself lucky.

If you are at home and not lying in a hospital, consider yourself lucky.

If you have friends to call up, consider yourself lucky.

Just write down all the positive experiences you had and all the sweet memories.

Automatically, in 10 mins, you will feel good, and for all those blessings, say thanks to the universe.

I tell you a story of Prophet Musa centuries ago; people believed that he can have a conversation with God. One day, a humble billionaire met with Prophet Musa and told him that he already has enough wealth. The next time if he has any conversation with God, please tell God not to bestow him any wealth. The Prophet nodded, okay. The next day, a beggar met with Musa and asked him why, if his God is kind enough, he hasn't showered any blessings on him. Please tell Him to bring me enough wealth that I can believe that there is someone up there. Musa agreed.

The next day, Musa had a conversation with God. He asked God to have mercy on the beggar and stop giving blessings to the billionaire.

The god replied, both the wishes will be fulfilled soon. Just tell the billionaire to stop being thankful for the blessings and tell the beggar to start being thankful for the blessing he has.

The next day, the prophet met the billionaire and asked him not to be grateful for the blessings he is receiving from God. The humble billionaire replied that it's impossible for him not to be grateful for what God is offering to me. It's my courtesy. I'm so sorry, Musa, I couldn't ignore the blessings which I am receiving from God for a long time. Musa smiled and said, with this attitude, it's impossible for you to be deficient of wealth.

The next day, the prophet met the beggar and advised him to start counting his blessings; his sorrows will vanish with time. The beggar laughed at Musa and asked, "Counting this small cloth, stale food? I think your god is not kind. I don't believe you had a meeting with God," and he walked away. The prophet understands the difference in the attitude of both men.

So whatever you have with you, always be grateful. Gratitude is the best form of attitude. When you wake up in the morning, say thanks to the almighty. There are many who couldn't wake up to see the morning. Start practicing the attitude of gratitude for the small things you have, and soon the universe will fulfil you with abundance.

Gratitude is a powerful practice of acknowledging and appreciating life's blessings. It shifts focus from what's lacking to what's abundant. Gratitude, in many ways, strengthens relationships, improves mental health, fosters resilience, encourages kindness, and increases happiness.

A daily habit of reflecting on blessings, writing a gratitude journal, sharing thanks to people around us and the universe, and appreciating nature's beauty can cultivate the attitude of gratitude in oneself.

3

GOOD DEEDS BOOMERANG BACK

"Cultivating the habit of good deeds will not only affect those around us, it will improve our own emotional well-being."

– Debbie Macomber

Baba, is it true that good deeds come back to you, Multifoods?

Of course, Raghav, I am a strong believer of this fact.

I tell you a real story from around a century ago.

There was a poor farmer named Fleming in Scotland. He lived there with his family in a village. One day, while working in the field, he heard the cry of a boy in a nearby bog. He quickly ran to the bog, and what he saw was a boy screaming and struggling to free himself from black muck.

Fleming saved the boy from a slow and terrifying death and dropped him safely at his nearby home.

The next day, in the morning, an elegantly dressed nobleman arrived at his home in a luxurious car and knocked on Father Fleming's door.

Oh, Mr. Fleming, I am the father of the pity boy you saved last night from the bog. I am extremely thankful to you and want to pay you for your kind gesture. Please let me know, "What I can do for you in exchange for this great help?"

Oh sir, I did nothing great. It was my humble duty at that time, and God wanted me to perform that. Anyone else would have done the same.

At the same time, a small child arrived home after playing in the garden.

"Oh, Mr. Fleming, is he your child?" "Yes, sir,"replied Fleming with a smile on his face.

"Doesn't he go to school?"

"I am sorry; sir, but he helped me on my farm. We cannot afford school."

The nobleman replied, "Please let me make a deal for you."

"Please let your son accomplish the same level of education as my own son."

The poor farmer cried with love and respect in his eyes, letting God decide his destiny.

The poor farmer Fleming's son attended the very best school of that time, graduated from a profound medical college in London, and became a renowned scientist, Sir Alexander Fleming, the discoverer of the medicine penicillin.

Years later, the same rich nobleman's son, who was saved from the bog in childhood, was stricken with a life-threatening disease, pneumonia, and his condition was getting worse with time.

Then occurred the lord's repayment. His life was saved with the introduction of the drug penicillin, which was discovered by the poor farmer's son.

The name of the nobleman was Rudolf Churchill, and his son's name was Winston Churchill, the former prime minister of the United Kingdom.

So, it's a real story that proved that nature repays you for your good deeds.

Our good deeds come back to us in many ways. Sometimes as miracles, sometimes as a shield, and sometimes as blessings upon our kids.

By doing good, we enhance our well-being, build stronger communities, cultivate empathy, and experience joy. The law of karma reminds us that every act of kindness returns multiplied. So spread love, compassion, and generosity.

As Mahatma Gandhi said, "The best way to find you is to lose yourself in the service of others."

4

LIVE MINIMALISTIC

"Have nothing in your house that you do not know to be useful or believe to be beautiful."

– William Morris

Baba, how do you manage to live with very few things? Don't you miss materials for your living?

Raghav, do you feel more airy in my house? Yes, Baba, really.

Raghav, I have learned that true happiness and fulfilment come not from accumulating possessions, but from living simply and appreciating what truly matters. I've learned to appreciate the essentials like food, shelter, love and health. Find joy in experiences like nature, laughter and relationships. To value memories over materials like cherishing moments, not objects. I always preferred to live minimally in my life. I have seen many people accumulate a lot of materials in their houses, making them look like storage units. I feel that when a house is filled with more and more goods, you lack fresh air to breathe. So, I always prefer not to collect more items in my house.

I believe that living minimally simplifies your life and helps you focus more on buying quality, not quantity. It prevents you from being dependent on things for your survival, and less quantity also makes your survival easier.

I have read somewhere that all things absorb energy. When the things are new, they contain positive energy, and when they get old, they fill with negative energies. Enough of negative energy in the goods breaks them into pieces when their time is over, like human beings. Your new air conditioner also has a certain age, your new car also has an age, your clothes will also get torn or fade with time; nothing lasts forever. Meanwhile, we get them repaired, like we cure a patient with medicines. Every non-living thing also has a certain age; beyond that age, we shall get them replaced. New things bring new joy and also help to boost the country's economy as well.

I have made a habit of decluttering every now and then. Whenever I buy any new item, I give away the old one that I already have, to someone in need. When I buy a new pair of clothes, I donate the old ones. Likewise, for the entry of any new item, the old item has to leave its place. This way, I get rid of items that I no longer need or use. Before buying anything, I ask myself whether I have space for it in my house.

I always love to accumulate experience over material possessions, by travelling more and more to new places.

By the process of decluttering, I have very few things to maintain; therefore, I have to spend very little on home maintenance. I have experienced that our older generations have bonded their emotions with materials and properties. The reason behind it is that in those times, it was very difficult to obtain those possessions. They had to try hard to save money, sacrifice some other things to obtain those precious materials, so their minds don't allow them to easily get rid of those possessions. They don't discard those materials easily, even after getting new items.

But today, with increasing per capita income, it's not that difficult to buy more than one pair of shoes. It's not tough to have more than 4 pairs of clothes; we feel free to change our mobile phones in a couple of years. So, we need to declutter things from the house and not get too much attachment to materialistic things. In today's time, it's not very difficult to get them back.

Decluttering is a practice that teaches us not to attach too much to things, since things don't exist for a lifetime. Over time, the value of things decreases, and new upgrades should be welcomed. Additionally, you can donate old items to the needy; in this way, you passively engage in some social service. By decluttering, you keep yourself organised in a logical way. There is also an 80/20 rule which states that 80% of the time you will only use 20% of your belongings, so you only need to keep those 20% of items. Also, when you have fewer materials, you need less time to search for them. A clutter-free space helps you concentrate and stay focused on tasks.

To live minimally, you need to differentiate between your needs and wants.

Needs are things we need to live and survive, but wants are things we would like to have, but we don't need to live. Needs are basically food, shelter, and clothes, but wants are expensive smartphones, luxurious perfumes, wristwatches, and many more. Our needs are limited and consist of not more than 30 percent of our expenses; the rest 70% are merely our wants and desires.

Desires don't have any limit and many a time contagious. If you find your neighbour or friend buying a new car, you also desire to get a new car like them. If your friend has a Gucci or Louis Vuitton bag, then your mind urges you to have them. If your friend buys a 4 BHK premium flat, you also want to buy that flat to match the circle. This attitude sometimes kills your hard-earned money and puts you in loan or debt. You need to have control over your desires if you want to live a minimalist life, and there is nothing wrong in it.

Baba, in order to achieve more success in less time, can we turn our desires into needs?

Well, Raghav, it's a very important and useful concept. It's always said that your need outweighs your desires, or you can say that your compulsions weigh more than your wants.

To achieve more success in less time, try to convert your wants into necessity. For example, you know that doing physical exercise is good for your health and you want to do it, but many times you feel lethargic to start or you don't get a kick from inside. However, if you make it a necessity, there is a strong possibility that you will perform it on a daily basis.

You desire to make a fixed study routine for the whole year, but most of the time, you tend to study seriously one month before exams and even harder on the day before exams since it's a necessity.

To convert your desires into necessity, you need to identify the WHY behind it. A strong why will be able to convert your want into need. You need to identify the benefits of achieving your desires that will improve your life. Proper planning and consistent efforts are needed to achieve your wants. Also, you need to remind yourself why this desire is essential for you and why you should stay committed to make it a necessity. Making proper deadlines also makes a task a compulsion, and you develop a sense of urgency to create a sense of necessity.

Always remember that turning desires into needs requires dedication, hard work, and willingness to prioritise your goals. You need to develop an emotional connection to your desires; strong emotions like passion, determination, and excitement will transform your desires into compelling drivers.

5

TIMELESS TRUTHS FROM THE SAINT

"All of us must be saints in this world. Holiness is a duty for you and me, so let's be saints and give glory to the father."

– Mother Teresa

"Baba, you told me that you visited Uttarkashi to stay in a very ancient ashram. At that time, what was your experience?"

"Yes, Raghav, it was around 30 years ago when I visited Uttarkashi. At that time, there were very few hotels in Uttarkashi. I was fortunate to stay with Swami Shivanandan in his ashram. He was an 80-year-old saint at that time. He used to eat only once a day, and people remember him for his eternal wisdom and knowledge of truth.

He gave me 6 teachings, which I will give you today.

1. All your efforts you are doing in any work are getting recorded in the universe, and you will definitely get the reward of your hard work when the time comes, either in this life or in your next birth. Nothing goes in vain. If you are continuously doing good deeds or hard

work and you are not getting any results, don't just get tired and quit; everything you do is getting registered in the universe; you will get the fruits if not today, then tomorrow or in your next birth.

2. No one has come into this world to please you. Everyone is busy with their own journeys, fighting for their own survival, and taking care of their own priorities in life. Everyone wants their own growth. No one will take time to put themselves in your shoes, so never expect much from people around you. Expecting much will only make you sad. In fact, you should work hard to achieve your own goals in life.

   People are busy fighting their own battles. How can you expect them to make you happy and fulfilled? Don't be so demanding; try to live minimally. Your happiness and fulfillment depend on you, not on others. You should learn to accept people as they are, without trying to control them. Accepting this fact helps us to become responsible for our own growth and self-improvement. It helps us focus more on the positive aspects of our relationships and express thanks for the love and support we receive from people around us.

3. He advised me to never share the knowledge of your income with anyone. Many people don't want you to grow. Sharing your income information will not give you any benefit, though it can sometimes attract evil eyes. I have seen many men who don't share their income information even with their family members, and there is nothing wrong with it.

4. He advised me to never share your past mistakes with any of your friends; there is no sense in doing that. You might not have the same relations with your friend throughout your life, and it can be misused by him. Don't become an open book even to your near and dear ones. Don't share about your past relationships with your present spouse also; sometimes it can ruin your family life too.

5. He advised me to never share your strengths and weaknesses with any person; people can take advantage of your weaknesses against you. Also, don't let your partner know that he/she is your weakness and that you can't live without them, or else your partner will not value you. You should not be dependent on anyone for your survival.

6. He advised me to never ever show off your donations. Whenever you donate, one hand should not let the other know about it. Do not donate just to get public attention; donations should always be kept secret.

6

NO COMPARISONS, JUST GROWTH

"When you are content to be simply yourself and don't compare or compete, everybody will respect you."

– Lao Tzu

Baba, I have seen that many a time's people are jealous of each other. They think that the other person's life is better, going on and always compare them with others. How to deal with this comparison disorder?

See, Raghav, its human tendency that, by default, he compares himself with another person's quality of life. I believe every human creature is unique and important. No one is worthless in this world. All have 2 hands, 2 legs, the same body organs, and the same biological brain.

But, the thinking pattern and mindset of all individuals are different.

Sometimes we think that a particular fellow who is richer or more successful, or who has topped in college has a more sound brain, but it's not true. He may have higher intellect, but it's not necessary that he has a more dynamic brain than you. So never underestimate yourself in life.

Let me explain it to you in simpler language. Suppose we divide the brain into 10 equal parts. These parts can be named as the intellectual mindset part, business mindset part, social mindset part, peaceful mindset part, aggressive mindset part, artistic mindset part, communication mindset part, technical mindset part, service mindset part, and many more.

We can assume that a person who is good in technology may be using more of his technical mindset, so with time, his technical motor functions of the brain become stronger. An artist who is not good in technology may be using his artistic part more, so his artistic motor functions have evolved more with time. A good businessman is using that part of the brain which is inclined more towards business skills; he may not be good in arts or technology. Many of the politicians and leaders are using that part of the brain that is inclined more towards socialising. Artists and poets are using another part of the brain, so they may not be good at socialising.

Likewise, when you see that a person who is low-profile and not wealthy may be better at socialising skills than the person who is richer.

So, all men are unique in their own ways. It is also possible that a fellow who is very high-profile and rich with huge material possessions may be lonely and sad inside. Happiness and contentment, part of the brain, have nothing to do with wealth and success. It is true that the rich can enjoy more facilities and luxuries, but a high happiness index is not guaranteed with it.

So never underestimate anyone who is not in a higher post. That person may be superior to you in some other motor brain functioning, yet scientists have to make a lot of discoveries in brain programming. It may be true that a millionaire may not be enjoying a sound sleep because that contentment part of the brain is not strong, while a poor truck driver may enjoy a sound sleep after getting into bed in a few minutes. So no one is worthless; God has made all of us different. Never compare yourself with anyone; comparison should be done only with oneself.

Happiness is a practice, not a destination. Many times I have noticed that people with ample financial resources may lack meaningful relationships, feeling isolated despite their riches. Individuals with strong family ties and friendships may struggle financially, wishing for stability. And those who seem to have both wealth and loving relationships may face health challenges. So appreciate what you have, and focus on blessings, not lack. No one has it all; strive for harmony in all aspects.

7

REFINE YOUR CONNECTIONS

"I have learned that people will forget what you said, people will forget what you did, but people will never forget how you made them feel."

– Maya Angelou

"Baba, how come you were so busy yesterday? I saw you spending a lot of time on phone calls; your mobile was ringing throughout the day and even at night. What's the matter? Is everything alright? You were also calling many people. Please let me know about the matter. I think I can help you with it."

Vishwanath took a glass of warm water and smiled.

"See, Raghav, yesterday was the second Saturday. Every second Saturday, you will see me busy with my phone. Every second Saturday, I celebrate "well-being day" or in Hindi, you can call it "haal chal pucho day."

On this day, I call up 3 people whom I never talk to often and ask about their well-being.

How is their health? How is everything going on in their life? Where are they now? How are their children doing?

I have maintained this habit for the last 15 years. Many people are motivated to practice this habit. I call them, they call me, they call others, and others call me. I get dozens of phone calls on this day.

Yes, Baba, this practice seems interesting. Tell me in detail. I also want to develop this custom of calling my contacts on this day.

Actually, it was around 15 years ago when we got mobile phones in our life. One day, I was busy taking a shower. At that moment, I got this idea of spending one day in a month to just speak with our relatives, friends, or any person whom we have met in life and got their mobile numbers.

With time, we get busy in our life. We hardly have time to polish our relations by visiting them. So, I got this idea to dedicate a few minutes in a month to speak to our relatives / friends who are not in touch, and on that day, it was the second Saturday of that month.

If you want to cultivate this habit, just mark one day of the month. Saturday or Sunday will be fine because people have holidays on this day. Just choose a minimum of 3 people. It can be 5 or 7, depending on how free you are, but normally in the beginning 3 are sufficient.

Try to call them in the morning around 9 am, not before that. Some people like to sleep more on holidays. Most people feel fantastic when you wish them good morning. Ask them about their well-being, health, and their children's education. Their charm remains throughout the day. Just give at least 2-3 minutes; it will hardly take more than 15 minutes in a month. You will feel good each time, your contacts will improve, your vocabulary will expand, and of course, your good-luck will increase.

"Baba, how come fortune will be improved?"

"Raghav, I believe many times luck is related to opportunities. If you go to meet people, you open doors of opportunities for you, but if you have no time to go and meet, you can still call them up on the phone."

"I advise you never to ask for help in terms of money when you develop this habit; otherwise, people won't like it. It should be a casual talk asking for their well-being, not for our own interests. Believe me, this habit will be a great tool for nurturing your relations and contacts. After a few months, you would like to be connected to people; just 15 minutes in a month will create a big impact on your relations. It will also help you to improve your communication skills. Always try to value others because the value you add to someone's life decides your place in their life."

While talking to them, take their names. People like to hear their name, so try to use it more often. During discussions, invite them to your home and also plan to meet them if they invite you; it will make you more social. You can choose your preferred time, whether morning or evening, but never call when you are driving a vehicle or the other person is driving or busy elsewhere. If someone is suffering from an illness or feeling low, you can visit them if they are near your place.

Be the reason someone feels seen, heard, loved, appreciated, safe, supported, valued, and less alone. Be the one who makes others feel included.

"In the beginning, you will find this habit troublesome, but believe me, after 2 months, you will wait for this day. Our mind opposes any new change, but after some time, it adapts to the change automatically. Many times, we assume that the other person must be very busy and we should not disturb them, but if someone has seen your WhatsApp status, he's not that busy, Raghav."

"Baba, I promise you that from this month, I will add this good habit in my life."

8

DON'T BLAME THE UNIVERSE, DESIGN YOUR DESTINY

"One of the basic rules of the universe is that nothing is perfect. Perfection simply doesn't exist. Without imperfection, neither you nor I would exist."

– Stephen Hawking

Baba, sorry to ask you, but how did you cope with the event of the accident of your child (my father and mother, and your wife)? How were your emotions? How did you spend your time after that event? Don't you feel that God has been unfair to you, that there is no one to look after you in your old age?

Old age? Who is old? I don't consider myself old. Time has gifted me with invaluable experience, making me a master of my craft. Some days I feel sad about the demise of my son, wife, and daughter-in-law, but after one month, I met one of my friends, Rajendra. He told me something interesting that helped me come out of my sadness.

He told me that nothing is permanent in this world, everything is temporary. Every life has a predetermined expiration date, and we have to accept it.

He told me that there are a certain number of mathematical probabilities of accidents, congenital defects, divorce rates, breakups, cheats, or any other uncertain miseries in this world since ages, and we have to accept that. Most of that is less than 0.5 percent out of a hundred, and for that, we should never blame any unknown source for our sufferings.

When we don't know the cause of suffering, we tend to blame unknown sources and nature. Miss happenings are not in our hands, so why think like that? Accidents are just a matter of chance, but suffering from them is the matter of choice.

Some people think that God is unfair to them. They consider themselves unlucky, thinking that they were born on a wrong date, so their astrological charts are not strong, and they have to suffer from it throughout their life.

But believe me, it's not like that. Everything is a game of mindset and attitude. A negative mindset attracts negativities in life. I always believe that God and astrology can give you cards, but it's up to you how you play with those cards. I have seen in my life some people born with good cards who cannot play well and remain losers, while some people born in small towns, poor families with the worst cards play very well the game of life and come out as winners.

So you only have choices, and your choices define your destiny. If you think positively, you will attract positivity, so always be thankful for what God has offered you and always remain in a state of gratitude. In fact, you can help others who are suffering; then you will realise that your sufferings are very less.

My daily exercise, good sleep, positive attitude, and feeling of gratitude have helped me a lot in coming out of this unfortunate incident, along with these practical steps which were taught to me by my friend Rajendra:

1. Allow emotions, don't suppress.
2. Seek support from family, friends or professionals.
3. Take care of basic needs (food, sleep, hygiene).
4. Create rituals.
5. Share memories and stories
6. join a support group
7. Travel
8. Cultivate gratitude and seek counselling.

Shift your perspective:

From "why me" to "what can I learn from it?"

From blame to self-awareness.

From victimhood to empowerment.

9

EMPOWERING HABITS

"In a nutshell, your health, wealth, happiness, fitness, and success depend on your habits."

–Joanna Jast

Baba, sometimes I don't find my mind stable. Last year on New Year, I went to the gym did heavy workout from day one but after one week, I discontinued it. And now, I don't dare to go back to the gym again. I want to cultivate the habit of going to the gym, but I don't feel that motivation inside me. What do you suggest? Is there any way to develop good habits easily?

Raghav, I believe more than 70% of youth feel the same. But today, I will give you a trick to develop good habits easily. The human mind is genetically designed to conserve energy from the time of evolution. When we think of starting any new task, our mind looks at it as a bulk task and, to save your energy, it discourages you to start it.

So my motto is whenever you like to start any new project, in the beginning, you just do one thing... "Start small."

Tomorrow, if you want to go to the gym, just don't plan for a workout. In fact, plan to get up, go to the gym, and come back without doing any exercise. The most difficult task is to get out of bed and reach the gym, but not workout. For a few days, just go to the gym, meet the trainer, take some information, and come back. Then, after some days, start by doing small physical exercises, like 5 minutes on the treadmill, and come back. By doing this, you are training your mind to accept this change, and that's most important. If you want to start meditation, begin by sitting for just 2 minutes at first, and gradually increase your time day by day. If you want to write a book, start by writing 2 lines initially, then one paragraph, and then a page. In this way, your mind will not oppose you.

Have you heard about the moment of inertia in school?

It means that when the body is at rest, it will tend to remain at rest until, and unless, some external force is applied to it. When the body is in motion, it will continue to be in motion until any external force is applied to stop it.

So, if you want to break that inertia, in order to start something new, it's only in the beginning that your mind and body will oppose you. Whenever you feel like procrastinating for any task, just divide the task into bits and act on it; your job will be half done. Start by being slow and be consistent. You can achieve anything in your life if you start bit by bit and are consistent with it. In the beginning, everything looks tedious and giant, but when you start to act on it, your mind and body help you complete that work. And it only takes around 2 months to develop a new habit; some say its 21 days. But I believe its 2 months.

I particularly believe that your habit designs your destiny. If you possess a habit of getting up early in the morning and doing some physical exercise, eating less processed food and sugar, you automatically possess a disease-free life in the future. One more thing I must tell you is that in order to stay young, always try to learn something new and give challenges to your body and mind. After a certain age, we all tend to prefer living in a comfort zone and avoid trying new things, but it's also true that there is no growth in a comfort zone.

Baba, there are some people who know that they are indulged in the bad habit of excessive smoking and drinking alcohol, but they find themselves helpless to get out of that habit. How to leave those habits which are injurious to our own health?

Always remember, Raghav, where there is a will, there is a way. They have to work on it. We become what goes into our mind: good in, good out; garbage in, garbage out; positivity in, positivity out; negativity in, negativity out.

If you can control the kind of association you are living in, it can influence your future by automatically creating good habits. Just watch your thoughts; your thoughts become your words. Watch your words; your words become your actions. Your actions create habits, your habits form your character, and your character creates your destiny. So always try to create good associations in your life. Always remain in the company of good friends and people. **I strongly believe that you are the average of the 5 people you spend most of your time with**. So choose your company wisely.

Your income, health, respect, and thinking pattern are average of 5 people you spend most of your time with. So, it's necessary that your friends and family members have good habits. You can join any good club in your town that has members who are successful and having positive mindset that you want to develop.

I always believe that one thing that can change your destiny is your MINDSET. Yes, Mindset is everything.

Now, I will tell you 3 good habits which I think you should develop that will improve your life gradually.

1. **Physical Exercise:** If you invest your time in doing any sort of physical activity like aerobic, strength training, yoga, zumba, jogging, running, walking, etc., then you will get returns throughout your life. If you have a gym nearby, you can join; otherwise, you can easily do your workouts at home. Do at least 5 days a week of workout, and you will see a clear transformation in your body and mind. If anyone has a habit of smoking, it will reduce the craving of smoking gradually, and you will end up leaving the habit of smoking and alcohol. It will help you get better sleep, which will automatically improve your productivity and definitely give rise to promotion in your company. It will improve your digestion and metabolism, and you will like to add nutritional food into your diet. By eating better and sleeping better, you will definitely look good and feel more confident. It will take around a year for you to acquire a drastic positive transformation. If you are already exercising, then never ever quit this habit, come what may, at any cost.

2. **Better Sleep:** If you get proper sound sleep of around 7-8 hrs, you will feel more energetic and able to concentrate better in your work. Your body heals itself during sound sleep. Try to sleep before 10 pm at night; the earlier you sleep, the deeper you sleep. Sleep deprivation gives rise to stress, which causes various ailments like depression, hypertension, thyroid disorders, diabetes,

and many more. Your hormones like testosterone and oxytocin work well if you get good sleep. Going to bed early can help you rise earlier in the morning, allowing you to start your day sooner. You will have more time to complete tasks.

3. **Meditation:** It's a practice which involves a technique to focus the mind on a particular object, thought, or activity to increase awareness and achieve a clear and calm state of mind. Most of our religious saints were following this technique from traditions to achieve peace of mind. It has tremendous benefits in lowering stress and achieving calmness. It relaxes your mind to gain hyper-focus in your work and increases concentration power. A wandering mind decreases output in your work. In the beginning, you can start by sitting for 5 minutes daily to meditate, preferably in the morning on an empty stomach. If you know nothing about meditation, just sit and focus on your breath. In the beginning, your mind will wander; let it be, it's normal. Gradually increase your time for it.

A strong body and a strong mind will always take you high in spirits.

Now, I will tell you about 2 destructive habits which make a man poor over time.

1. **Addiction:** Addiction may be of sugar, cigarette, alcohol, mobile, porn, drugs. All these things gradually destroy you from inside. It starts very slowly, but gradually its frequency increases. And of course, good habits need energy and effort to develop, but bad habits don't need any effort to grow. These bad habits are pleasurable, but

they lower your energy to focus on important activities of life. I have seen people destroying their family life because of excessive alcohol addiction. Never ever become the slave of any bad habit. If you want to leave any of your addictions, don't hesitate to visit a counsellor.

2. **Bad Company:** As I have told you earlier, you are the average of the 5 people you spend most of your time with, so make sure you spend time with the right kind of people. People who are not ambitious and have a negative attitude are contagious. Try to be aware of your associations; avoid frequent smokers, alcoholics, and backbiters. Always join the company of friends who are ambitious and serious about their future. Make friends with people who read good books. Choose your company carefully.

10

SCHOOLS DESERVE RESPECT

"The capacity to learn is a gift, the ability to learn is a skill, and the willingness to learn is a choice."

– Brian Herbert

Baba, your great grandson Yuvam is not doing well in maths these days, and I think his maths teacher is not working hard on him, and the entire school is not taking care of school children in studies. Should I change the school?

See Raghav, what I believe is if you don't like any particular school, you always have an option to change schools. But one important piece of advice I will give you is never to say any negative sentences about school and school teachers in front of your child, even if you dislike that teacher and the school.

Sometimes parents don't like any school's teacher. If they are dissatisfied with a school teacher, they start speaking negatively about that teacher to others in front of their children. Your child is listening to everything you say, and he starts disliking that teacher. When he doesn't like the teacher, he won't respect them, and sooner or later, he will lose interest in that subject. So always show respect to school teachers in front of your children. Whatever complaints you have about any school, address them politely with the school management and the teacher themselves. Always remember, the child will learn best from the teacher who has the best image in the child's mind.

Once my Sanskrit teacher, Mr. Narendra, told me in my school days that whatever faith and admiration you have for a teacher, the same kind of knowledge and beliefs you will receive from him. So never ever complain about any school teacher in front of your child. And sometimes when your child complains about any teacher, make him aware that they are working very hard for your betterment.

Until and unless there is some serious issue, like physical torture, don't be judgemental about a school teacher.

Teachers are mentors and sometimes should be treated as role models for students. You are not aware of the challenges they face to meet your expectations. You should always respect their dedication and hard work. Also, you should always express gratitude for their service.

Teachers are also human beings; they also need moral support and motivation to complete their tasks in the given time.

Baba, what does a teacher expect from a student? And what does a student expect from a teacher?

Well, Raghav, a teacher more or less looks for these 4 qualities in a student. You could say that if a student possesses these 4 qualities, he or she can become the favourite student of a teacher.

1. **Respect –** the first and foremost thing a teacher wants from a student is respect. A student who doesn't respect his teacher can never become a favourite for his teacher,

and having respect and showing respect are 2 different things. If you have respect for your teacher, then automatically it will reflect in your actions. Although a teacher should also try his best to earn respect from students, and that's possible if you care for your students and personally satisfy every student.

2. **Punctuality and participation** - punctuality doesn't exist without discipline, so a well-disciplined student always catches the eyes of a teacher. The teacher needs you to be attentive in class; he needs you to take part in discussions. You should be present in class both mentally and physically. You should participate in asking questions. Asking intellectual questions shows your intelligence. Asking questions shows that you are listening carefully to the topic in the class. A teacher feels motivated if the student looks at the face of the teacher at the time when he is speaking. If the teacher is jolly by nature, he will always like the smiling face of students.

3. **Faithfulness and honesty** - you should be truthful and honest in your academic work. Being sincere in projects and completing tasks on time creates a positive impact on the teacher. Following classroom rules and maintaining decorum in class is much more appreciated by a teacher. Some teachers like students who dare to sit in the first row. Since it needs confidence to sit there, because it demands much more attentiveness. Completing assignments on time also makes a good impression on your teacher's eyes.

4. **Curiosity –** being curious to gain knowledge and learning new things is always a sign of a good student. You should always maintain a habit of curiosity. A child is born with this habit to always ask questions about each and every thing he experiences to his parents and teachers, but with time, this habit is forcefully withdrawn by his parents and teachers. Both parents and teachers should never discourage a child from askingquestions. In fact, they should take patience and appreciate his curious nature, or else the child will lose this habit with time during his growth phase.

A good teacher will never discourage this habit of a student and will always listen to questions asked by his students patiently. Innovative ideas are always born in curious minds. A curious student will always have a genuine interest in learning.

By meeting these qualities, any student can build positive and strong relationships with his teacher, and it helps in cultivating a sound learning environment.

Now, Baba, can you tell what a student expects from a teacher? What qualities are needed to become the favourite teacher of students?

Well, I always believe that for a person, before becoming a good teacher, he has to become a good human being who likes to serve people with his knowledge and develop a sense of encouragement for others.

A good teacher will more or less have these 4 qualities,

1. **Expert and passionate** - he should be an expert in that field; people respect a knowledgeable person. He should have a core understanding in that particular field.

He should be interested in never-ending learning in that field and always find time to update himself in that field. Today, the world is full of competition even for a teacher; constant updating in the field is a necessity.

Teaching is a noble profession that shapes the character, intellect, and souls of future generations. St. Elizabeth Seton.

2. **Positive attitude and motivation** - if the teacher is positive, the students feel safe with him. A teacher should always motivate students to learn; it is one of the best qualities of a teacher. Many times students fail in exams or are unable to clear competitive exams. A teacher with a positive attitude and good motivational qualities can always encourage students during setbacks. Student suicides due to excessive study pressure and depression are at their highest these days. Therefore, a teacher with good motivational qualities and a calm mental attitude can work wonders in their lives.

3. **Clear explanations** - a teacher should have the quality to convert difficult and complicated concepts of subjects into simple explanatory concepts, thereby making it easier to understand. Teaching in a playful manner reduces the boredom between students.

4. **Never make fun of weak students -** a good teacher never humiliates weak students and never discourages them in front of other students. In fact, he tries to work hard and put in extra efforts to uplift weak students. It takes nothing great to uplift intelligent students, but it requires extra efforts and true potential for a teacher to show his calibre in uplifting weak students. No 2 students are the same in terms of learning ability, so

never underestimate any weak student and accept them as they are. I have seen in my life that many weak students have achieved higher positions later in their lives. It is the prime responsibility of a teacher to encourage each and every student. Sometimes, the insult or any negative comment made by a teacher to a weak student imprints in the mind of the student for a lifetime, impacting negatively on the self-confidence of that student.

Better than a thousand days of diligent study is one day with a great teacher, a Japanese proverb.

11

HOLD MEMORIES IN YOUR HANDS

"What I like about photographs is that they capture a moment that is gone forever, impossible to reproduce."

– Karl Lagerfeld

"Hey Baba, I have noticed that you always lay emphasis on creating good memories. You remember a lot of your old memories. You always say that creating great memories is equal to creating a great life. But Baba, how do you manage to remember so much? Can you share any method of retaining those old memories so that they remain fresh?"

"Yeah Raghav, I will share a secret that I have been following for the last 10 years."

We all have smartphones where we take pictures. However, when we change our phones, let's say in 2 to 4 years, most of our pictures get deleted. Sometimes, we download them to our laptop or our new smartphone, where they remain without being noticed very often.

So, for the last 10 years, I have been making a hard copy album (similar to those made for weddings) of around one hundred selected pictures each year. About 20 years ago, we used to have such albums when we used Kodak or Canon cameras and Konica or Fujifilm reels...

Each year, in the month of December, I select around 10 pictures (sometimes more or less) from every month in my mobile gallery. This totals around 120 pictures for the year, which is more than enough to create a hard copy album for the year. I then give these pictures to a printing lab that creates an album from them.

So I have 10 albums of the last 10 years with me. Believe me, hard copies are better than soft copies. During the night, I sometimes see those albums, and it rejuvenates my mind.

Creating a hard copy album is a beautiful way to retain memories and cherish special moments. gather photos, mementos from meaningful events, trips, or milestones. Organise them chronologically, adding captions for contexts. Choose a sturdy album with acid free paper to ensure longevity. Adorn with stickers or artwork for a personal touch. Flipping through the pages, you will relive memories and emotions. Share with loved ones or treasure for generations to come. In the era of digital overload, a physical album offers a tactile, sentimental experience, preserving memories for years to come.

Baba, this is indeed a great concept of album making and saving old memories safely. I will surely make my hard copy album this year.

12

THE MINDSET

"Our greatest glory is not in ever failing, but in rising every time we fail."

– Confucius

Baba, when I look back at my life, I feel that some days are good, some are not good, and some are devastating. I feel that time is not always the same. Like in cricket matches, we say that a player is not in form these days. There are many ups and downs in life. How to handle these kinds of scenarios?

See, Raghav, you want to ask, "What should I do when I feel that my time is not good these days?" right?

Well, Raghav, I must say that these kinds of things come in everyone's life. Time is not constant every time. Sometimes we feel mood swings, we like to sleep more in the morning, have low energy levels, don't like to put extra efforts in work, don't like to dress up smartly, experience frequent irritations from small events, don't like to meet friends and relatives, like to spend more time alone, have frequent diseases, don't like to put in hard work, and don't like to take new challenges.

If more than a few things happen like this, then one can assume that the time is not good. But it's a great thing about the worst time that it always passes. After any worst phase in anyone's life, there comes a fair or good time, and it increases the value of good time. Times never remain the same in anyone's life, but when you are going through a tough phase, here's my advice.

And the answer is to **learn, learn, and learn**. Always handle your bad time with learning something new. Learning anything like any new subject, cooking, painting, computer language, communication skills, art and crafts, reading good books, joining any outdoor or indoor sports academy, dance classes, spend some time in the gym, learning a new language; any type of learning will work. In fact, you should read good books at that time.

There was a study conducted on the billionaires in the world, which found that 80% of the billionaires were first generations, and only 20% were second generations. When they were asked about their financial success, the answer was they read good books in their routine daily. They read a lot. Books help them to create ideas and imaginations. Reading sparks creativity, expands vocabulary, unleashes new ideas, and cultivates open-mindedness, transforming individuals into visionary leaders.

You know what Benjamin Barber, an eminent political theorist, once said: "I don't divide the world into weak and strong, or the successful and failures, I divide the world into learners and non-learners."

Zig Ziglar once said, "Failure is an event, not a person."

Everyone has their own viewpoint and perspective, and there is nothing wrong in it. The thought patterns of all individuals are not the same. *There is a famous quote from Shakespeare: "There is nothing either good or bad, but thinking makes it so."*

The tea you drink every day may be whisky for people of some other planet because both tea and whisky are addictive. We consider tea safe and normal, but who knows, people of some other planet may not take it as normal in their civilised society. Likewise, tribal people of some African countries do not wear clothes, and it's normal in their culture. But we, in our culture, do not accept it. We many a times measure success with material possessions owned by an individual, but who knows at some other planet they measure success with peace of mind, health and prosperity of an individual and not with possessions.

Who will decide what is wrong and what is right? We tend to develop an attitude and thinking pattern according to our upbringing in our society and culture.

Eating non-vegetarian food is not allowed in some religions, whereas it is allowed in various other religions. Everyone has their own perspective on things based on their religion, region, customs, and culture. So, it is important to respect people's opinions, or else you will create opposition for yourself. We have to put ourselves in their shoes and understand them.

"One day, you will tell your story of how you overcame what you went through, and it will be someone else's survival guide."
- Brene Brown

If you want to be young all the time, always spend some time on learning new things. You should always have a book reading habit. Learning new things keeps you busy and keeps your mind, body, and soul young. If you are a good learner, you will always feel positive and motivated in life. When you invest most of your time in learning during your worst times, you will receive the sweetest fruits in your good times. Also, when you learn something new, you can teach that thing to someone in need. Some of us are such advanced souls that we did not come here to be supported, but we came to be the support system for many. If you have had a challenging life and feel you never had support or love, that is because you are the love and support.

Always try to take on new challenges in life. Challenges are a part of life; the bigger the challenges, the bigger the growth. Always remember, when the question paper is tough in school examinations, chances are that the markings will be easy. If you feel like you don't fit in this world, it's because you are here to help create a new one.

So never be afraid to face tedious, hard tasks. If you manage to show guts to take tough tasks, the universe will help you overcome them in its own ways. Never ever be afraid to have setbacks and failures; without failures, you can't get tough in life. The universe prepares you for bigger projects by giving you failures and hardships.

Having a positive mindset is a powerful catalyst for success. Positive mindset itself doesn't bring the success, but it surely increases the probability of success. It empowers you to see challenges as opportunities, fostering resilience and growth. Imagine there are two persons starting to climb Mt. Everest. One is with positive mindset and damn sure that he will definitely conquer it and come back alive, and the other one is doubtful about it. What you think who have more chances of conquering it?

There are numerous emotional benefits of positive mindset:

1. Reduced stress and anxiety.
2. Improved mood and overall sense of well- being.
3. Increased resilience and coping skills.

4. Enhanced self-confidence and self-esteem

5. Better relationships and social connections.

There are numerous physical benefits of positive mindset:

1. Boosted immune system.

2. Lower blood pressure.

3. Improved sleep quality.

4. Reduced chronic pain.

5. Increased energy levels.

There are numerous mental benefits of positive mindset:

1. Improved focus and concentration

2. Enhanced creativity and problem-solving skills

3. Increased productivity and efficiency.

4. Better decision making and judgement

5. Reduced mental fatigue

Now, I will briefly explain to you about 2 new different concepts of mindsets.

1. Fixed mindset

2. Growth mindset

Fixed mindset believes that intelligence and abilities are innate and unchangeable. Sees challenges as threats to ego. Avoids failure, fearing it exposes inadequacy. Focuses on proving oneself rather than improving. Views success as an affirmation of inherent talent.

On the other hand, a growth mindset believes that intelligence and abilities can be developed through effort and learning. It embraces challenges as opportunities for growth, sees failure as a valuable learning experience, focuses on progress, persistence, and self-improvement, and views success as a result of hard work and resilience.

But the good part is, there can be a mindset shift that can transform your relationship with learning, goals, and setbacks, unlocking your full potential.

(Now you can directly move to the section 'Learning' of the final chapter "six pillars of holistic living" in continuation with this chapter, then continues with the next chapter.)

13

NURTURE RELATIONSHIPS

"Love is when the other person's happiness is more important than your own."

– H Jackson Brown

Baba, I, and Divina were living happily together when our marital relationship was new and warm, but soon after some years of marriage, we lost our charm in the relationship. Is there any way to get that charm back to life?

Well, Raghav, it happens in every relationship. There was a time when I and Pariniti (your grandmother) were losing charm in our relationship. We both were quarrelling with each other every day without any reason.

In the beginning of any relationship, everything works fine. Both partners love and care for each other. They share each and every incident that happened during the day. They like to sit together, eat together, and spend most of their time together. Hormones play a major role in this. Life looks beautiful when relationships are warm and fresh, but after some time, nothing remains the same.

Human nature demands personal space, yet we often fail to respect our partner's boundaries. Our mind crave novelty, growing bored with familiarity, As relationships mature, they can stagnate, leading to disappointment and frustration for both partners, The initial spark often fades, leaving attraction dulled.

As per my knowledge, the best phase of the relationship is the courtship period. When both partners love and care for each other. Both are living in different houses, there is space between them. The first thing the partner notices is the good morning message of the companion on the mobile phone, that needs to be replied to with "I miss you" with twinkling stars and a smiley. Happy hormones secrete in both the bodies.

By looking at your happy face, Raghav, during your courtship period, I reckoned that the journey is going fine from both sides. During courtship, you believe that your partner is premier and will remain the same throughout life.

When you achieve something special at your workplace, the first person you want to convey about the achievement to is your companion. Life seems to be flying in magical colours.

Every morning, you call up your partner and ask, "What did you have for breakfast?" You always question the universe, wondering why this person never arrived in my life earlier. Life seems so much more comfortable with him; that fellow becomes a necessity in life, without whom you are no one.

Anything bitter occurs at your workplace or home, you just call up to him, and that fellow strengthens you and makes you calm down by some loving magical words, and you think that all is well now.

Some heart-touching conversations, and then everything is on track, and your heart gets nourished. Whenever you are in doubt about any obscure things, you ask your companion, and he or she suggests a coherent plan. There is so much to talk, express on the phone that it seems you feel spellbound on the phone. You feel normal to talk for 2-3 hours, nonstop on your mobile.

There are many instances when you introduce materials in relations, you feel passionate about delivering gifts to your partner, and you never miss any chance to deliver gifts to your partner.

Then comes the time of marriage, the long wait to be united is now over. The association of 2 minds, 2 bodies, 2 families, 2 cultures, 2 traditions takes place. After the marriage, both partners are on cloud 9 for a year, love is in the air, warmth in the relationship, enjoying good food together, surprises at breakfast, long drives in the evening, good morning kisses, tight hugs after arriving tired from the workplace, charm is eternal in the faces of both. Hormone levels are at their peak, both partners enjoy each other's company, they plan vacations together, upload pictures of their honeymoon on social media, and enjoy romantic cuddling in winters. You now prefer the rainy season more. They both like to visit relatives' houses together, go shopping together, choose beautiful bedsheets and curtains for their room. You enjoy decorating your bedroom with candles, perfumes, and aromas coming to life. You want to spend every hour with your partner, having early morning tea with the newspaper, evening snacks, and eating lunch and dinner from one plate.

But suddenly, after a few years of marriage, that charm fades away. Exactly, Baba, these days, I have seen many married couples; they lack tuning in their relationship. Both don't like to spend time together after a certain age. Is there any psychological aspect behind that? How can we rekindle the same glory in our relationships?

"Well, Raghav, there are many reasons behind that.

One of my psychologist friends, Dr. Arnav, told me that the minds of both men and women run differently. A female wants someone to listen to them; they will share their problems with men. Females know their answers very well, but they want you to listen to their problems. Many times, they don't want you to provide straightforward solutions to their problems. On the other hand, a man is known for his solution-oriented skills. He always tries to give solutions and doesn't like to waste time listening to them.

You just need to listen to her problems. Don't try to solve their problems until and unless it's not asked of you. A woman wants someone who can give them some attention. Women need love, validation and support.

But on the other hand, when a man is not in a good mood, just give him some space, man needs independence and space, don't, again and again, ask him what is the problem? Men need trust and respect.

Just give him some time; he just needs some silence. Don't just think that he is neglecting you or trying to get away from you. He just needs to spend some time with himself, and you should respect his space.

A man seeks peace and encouragement. Whenever a man is facing troubles, challenges, hardships, failures, or setbacks, he always needs encouragement from his partner. He needs a partner who can motivate him in his hard times and dark phases of life. If a female shows trust in her man during his worst phase, then a man can challenge the whole world and will never think of losing such a partner."

"A great marriage is not when the 'perfect couple' comes together. It is when an imperfect couple learns to enjoy their differences." – Dave Meure

In spite of any fight in marital relations, never forget these 4 basic rules of good marital life:

1. Communication: Communication is the basic rule to safeguard any happy married life. Despite any major conflict in the relationship, never stop communication. Practicing proper communication, whether verbal or non-verbal, is key to a healthy marriage. Lack of these conversations will make you feel lonely and sad even though you are with your partner. Stress is a common issue among married partners. Proper conversations among partners help in reducing stress. Unresolved issues are sometimes irritable and affect social and mental health. Communication makes your partner understand you more and learn about your expectations and aspirations. Before going to bed, try to sort out any conflict by communicating. Research says that if you can live without communicating for 7 days, there are chances that the bond between both partners has weakened. Lack of communication shows a lack of caring. Try to be like small children; after some time, they forget what happened earlier and go to play together. Communication is, no doubt, the fuel of any relationship.
2. Respect: Respect weighs more than love, especially for males. Control your tongue; sometimes it's more

dangerous than a sword. Speaking politely, even in a conflict situation, is a sign of maturity. Try to respect your partner in front of his friends and other family members. Giving respect to your partner also indicates your own upbringing in childhood. Try to speak in a moderate tone to your partner, not too loud, not too slow. You must love and respect your partner in front of your child, or else your child will also not respect you. Also, try not to disrespect your partner's family members. Giving respect to your spouse is one of the best methods to prevent your child from feeling insecure.

3. Quality Times: Many relationships get ruined just because of a lack of time. There is no charm in your married life left if you lack giving time to your partner. Many times, a partner considers not giving proper time. In this scenario, you have to evaluate the reason behind it. Twice a year, plan a vacation with your partner so that you can spend quality time together. This will rekindle your relationship. The entry of a third person occurs in any relationship because you don't care about giving quality time to your partner.

4. Compromise: No good relationship occurs without sacrifice and compromises. It's also a great rule in maintaining friendship. It's beneficial to maintain peace and longevity in the marriage. Sometimes it's better to accept defeat in order to save a relationship. Compromises show commitment in a relationship. It shows respect for a partner's needs and desires. In the long run, it increases trust and mutual understanding. In relationships, many times, both partners have their own

opinions and differences in values and habits, and on these differences, conflicts arise. Respecting each other's differences should be given preference. Compromise helps to ensure that both partners' views are heard, and a mutually beneficial solution should be carried out.

Until and unless the partner is a narcissist, there is nothing wrong in a little bit of compromise.

Baba, what's a narcissist?

A narcissist is a person who has an inflated sense of their own importance, a deep need for admiration, and a lack of empathy for others. Many a time, he displays haughty and condescending behaviour, never accepts his own flaws and weaknesses, and becomes aggressive when confronted with criticism. He likes to crave attention and praise. He takes advantage of others to achieve his own ends. He is considered a toxic relationship partner.

Remember that everyone can exhibit some of these traits at some point in time, but a narcissist consistently displays these characteristics in his or her behaviour.

In most married couples, there occur 3 phases in relationships:

The first phase is the attachment phase; it's the beginning of any relationship. Both partners like to spend time with each other; they enjoy each other's company. They focus only on the positive sides of their partner, showing their best selves to each other. They both believe they are made for each other, giving top priority to their partner. They love, care for, and support each other.

Then comes the second phase, that's the conflict phase. Usually, it comes after one or 2 years of marriage. Both don't accept the differences between them. Both start judging each other, sometimes neglecting the company of their partner. Both start thinking that he or she is not the perfect partner for them and they could have waited a bit longer. Both advise their younger, single cousins and friends not to get married, or else their life will be ruined. Both start scolding their parents, questioning the choice of partner made for them, and why their family background wasn't checked. They start judging their partner's family and focus only on the negative sides of their partner. Sometimes they think that they are only living together for the sake of the child. It's the phase where most divorces take place.

Baba, is there any chance that if both the partners pass this phase, then the chances of separation are less?

Well, Raghav, there is a very high probability that if both partners somehow succeed in finishing this phase, then the probability of their separation minimises to a greater extent.

On completion of this phase, there comes the third phase when they realise their kids are grown up; now they need to plan for a better future. With age, both partners become experienced and mature. A man usually succeeds in building a good amount of corpus, which brings personal satisfaction for both partners. So, having patience in the second phase pays a lot in the near future. Also, they both become dependent on each other in these 10 years, thinking that life's not easy without the partner. They cultivate the habit of attending various family functions together. The role of both sides' parents is also crucial in this phase.

This last phase is the acceptance phase. It usually arrives after around 8-10 years of marriage. Both partners accept the differences between themselves. Most marriages are already settled in this phase. Both become busy with their kids' school studies and start planning their kids' future.

Baba, is this true that many a time marriages break because a partner starts judging the other partner?

Of course, Raghav, it's also one of the causes of separation.

It is very easy to judge anyone, until and unless you don't fit yourself in the other person's shoes. In this world, everyone is fighting their own battles. Before judging anyone, see the situation from all angles, see the scenario, and see the circumstances.

Patience also plays a very important role in protecting a relationship. Patience is when you are supposed to get mad, but you choose to understand. Happiness is having a partner who is also your best friend.

And one more thing, it is not enough to give love, care, and time only to the partner. You have to accept his family members and show equal love and care to them as well. Consider the partner's family members as your own family members.

Think like this: when you want to pass or score well in your 10th standard, it would not be enough if you score well in your favourite subject but fail in other subjects. In order to pass your exam, you need to get passing marks in each subject. Suppose your favourite subject is maths and you score full marks in maths, but that is not enough to pass the exam.

You need to attempt all the subjects and at least get passing marks in all the subjects, and if you are a good student, you will try to get distinction in all the subjects. In the same way, if you want to have a happy relationship with your partner, try to get a distinction sort of relationship with all the family members. You need to care for your partner's parents, brothers, sisters, and whole family as well. That will create a great impression of yours in your partner's eyes, and in your worst time, your relations with his family members will save your relationship with your partner. You will definitely get the return of investing your time on them. So, always consider the family as a whole.

Always remember that better relationships thrive on mutual respect, trust and open communication. Practice active listening, empathy and understanding. Validate each other's feelings and resolve conflicts constructively.

(Now you can continue to read section 3 Relationships of final chapter six pillars of holistic living. Then continue with the next chapter)

14

TRAVEL TO SEEK EXPERIENCE AND REKINDLE RELATIONS

"Once a year, go some place you've never been before."

– Dalai Lama

Baba, I know that you like to travel a lot. And for a long time, you have been travelling throughout India. What are the benefits of travelling? Please share your views on the benefits of travelling.

See, Raghav, I, and Pariniti were living together very happily when our relationship was warm and new, but soon after some years of marriage, we lost our charm in the relationship. We both started ignoring each other in every aspect of life. So, I decided to sleep on a different bed. Then I remember my friend Aman, who was working in a hotel as a hotel manager. He gave me advice about married life, which I will share with you today.

He told me that if you want to have a happy married life, then you should go on a long vacation once a year and many short trips in a year. It will produce vitamin L in your relationship, or else you will have a boring monotonous routine in your relationships. He told me that we, in our society, are not conditioned for frequent travelling; we don't dare much on spending money on travelling, but instead, we shall boost our country's economy by travelling.

I always believe that being qualified is different from being educated, and travelling educates you in many ways. I always believe that life itself is a journey, and we are born to travel. Our saints, influencers, prime minister, president, and many celebrities and millionaires travel very frequently, and they learn a lot by travelling.

I always believe that travelling makes you come out of your comfort zone. During travelling, we encounter many problems, and we learn how to tackle them. Sometimes you don't get good food to eat, sometimes you shiver in winters; sometimes you get stuck in traffic jams. All these things help to make you patient and adaptable in life.

One more thing, I believe that a person who never travels is like a frog dwelling in a well; he always remains in his comfort zone. Travelling makes you polite, and it develops one's communication and linguistic skills. During travelling, you come across a lot of new faces of different genera, and you need to talk to them. It helps you become an extrovert.

Travelling makes you open-minded. You get to know about different customs and religions, you meet new people, and you have to accept them with their own customs and thinking patterns.

I have seen that people who always have a holiday booked are 100% happier than those who don't. I always believe that one thing you would not be able to do easily when time passes by and you grow old, if at all you have more money, is travelling. So, travel and see the world when you are young.

There are many things to see while travelling. You have beaches, pilgrimages, mountains, valleys, forest adventures, local markets of crowded cities. You have a variety of destinations to see. Each one has its own importance. Clean beaches are good for relaxation with friends and families, and it is one of the favourite honeymoon destinations of many couples. You can have sea bathing and adventure sports. You can enjoy seafood with coconut water.

Many pilgrimage temples are located along rivers. You can let your stress flow like a river stream by ringing bells during evening aarti beside the river and lighting diyas in the evening, which transports you to a different world of spirituality.

Then, you can have a nice time enjoying the mountains. You get to experience adventure climbing, and the cool weather in the mountains eases you during hot summers. You get to see the glorious sunsets in the evening and the mesmerising valley view from various places. There are beautiful lakes in the hills where you can enjoy boat riding.

Baba, what if your partner or friends are not free to travel with you?

Then, you should go for solo trips.

Isn't solo travel a bit boring?

No, Raghav, it's all about mindset. I have had a lot of solo travelling in my life. One thing I am a bit sure of is that when you complete your solo trips, you are now a more confident person. It decreases your dependence on others, and you learn to manage everything by yourself. You interact with different people of different races; you get to know more about yourself by travelling alone. You feel relaxed at your own pace when you travel alone. There is no burden of getting up early and sleeping late at night. When you are alone, you have all the freedom.

But you are vulnerable to scams, so be careful and don't trust blindly upon strangers. I always used to carry very little luggage during my solo trips.

Let me share with you one of my many solo trips. It was in June 1999 when I went on a solo trip to Darjeeling. I arrived at New Jalpaiguri railway station, and just after getting out of the train, I was in a totally different environment with so much fresh air. The northeast citizens were very gentle and welcoming in nature. I took a cab from New Jalpaiguri to Darjeeling. The roads were very sloppy, and the greenery was mesmerising; the scenic beauty was astounding. I had never explored northeast India before that, and I was totally mesmerised by its beauty.

I enjoyed praying in peaceful monasteries, walking for miles on hills, breathing pollution-free air, having hot tea in silent nature, riverside maggi, and momos. I was at my own pace, free from monotonous life and work. I enjoyed horse riding on hills; watching the sunrise on Tiger Hill at 5.00 am was a breathtaking experience. I did yoga and meditation in a holistic centre for around 10 days, amidst the Alps of nature, and had very humble conversations with the sweet northeast people. They regard tourists as their gods. Every evening, I had a campfire at my place where I engaged in sweet conversations with the villagers, learning about their customs and culture; their polite nature just won my heart. I also spent time with Tibetan monks who trained my mind to detach at times from this physical world, surrendering to the feet of God, and meditating for hours. I practised yoga nidra, which was a very stress-relieving exercise. I had very light sattvic food for many days. I became fitter after that vacation. This trip made me mentally sounder and helped me become more helpful and humble in nature, as I had the company of such kind and loving people for around 2 weeks. I took life less seriously after that trip and started living in the present.

Baba, I don't know many native languages of different locations. What if I'm not able to communicate with them?

Raghav, every human understands the language of love, care, kindness, misery, and troubles, so don't worry if you don't know any native language; your mind will help you express things. You can also use Google translator for more language help, which we didn't have at that time.

Baba, I got to know from Dadi long back that you have covered 90% of tourist destinations in India, but only a few foreign countries. Why didn't you travel outside India?

Raghav, to tell you frankly, at that time, before 30 years, it was not easy to travel outside India. Getting a passport and visas were not easy. Flight tickets were also very expensive. I also lay emphasis on first covering your own country, then visiting other countries. Because when you spend in your own country, you boost your country's economy. So, be proud that when you travel in your own country, you are improving your country's economy.

In our country, I have seen people accumulating money but spending very little on leisure trips because they are conditioned that way from childhood. But I always believe that after reaching a certain portfolio corpus, you should start spending money either on yourself, your family, or for charity. I believe that money is a form of energy; it cannot be stored in one place for a long time. I have seen some financial planners motivating people to save more and more money, invest it, and spend very little on consumables, but I don't agree with them. I never believe in investing more than 50% of your monthly income because if everyone starts spending less and investing more, the economy of the country will be severely impacted. How will a shopkeeper pay the school fees of his children if you don't buy something from his shop? So, never regret buying expensive items because money should circulate to improve a country's economy.

Baba, this is off the topic. You are speaking about the economy, we were on travel mode. But I like this too.

Baba smiled and took a sip of green tea.

15

FREEDOM OF LIFE AND HAPPY CHEMICALS

"Freedom from desire leads to inner peace."

– Lao Tzu

Baba, many a time, I feel stressed out at work. I experience a lack of energy, mood swings, and lethargy. Perhaps, I believe that even after earning a satisfactory income, I don't feel good. I also don't get good sleep these days.

How did you deal with these kinds of conditions when you were in your early forties?

Raghav, I believe that you are not the only youngster who is dealing with these kinds of conditions. I think 60 percent of the world's population is dealing with this condition.

My friend Rajendra always used to tell me one thing, "For humans, when the stomach is empty, there is only one problem, but when the stomach is full, there are one hundred problems."

Our heart wants love, mind wants success, and soul wants peace.

What do you think so?

Yes, Baba, he seems to be saying true. So what to do now?

See, one thing I ask you today. What is the most important thing you are running for today?

Baba, I guess its success, and it comes with earning huge money. We all in this generation need a lot of money to achieve our goals, survive, and fulfil our needs.

Do you really think this is the answer?

Of course, Baba.

Let me ask you a question.

If I give you one million dollars and put you in a cage, you can't move out of that cage. You will get all your food and necessary items in that cage, but you can't open and move out of that cage. What would be your priority then?

Baba, my mind will get depressed, like a prisoner. What would I do with that money then?

I would desperately want freedom.

Exactly, Raghav, you are not running for money; you are running to get freedom of life. We often mistakenly believe that money is the ultimate goal. However, the true aspiration is freedom- the liberty to live life on our own terms.

On earth we measure success by reaching financial stability or professional achievement but who knows on some other planet success is measured by achieving peace of mind, better relationships or better health.

We need to rethink our values and priorities and consider alternative definition of success and strive for balance and stress free holistic well- being.

This freedom can be autonomy to pursue passions, time for loved ones and personal growth, liberation from stress and anxiety, ability to make choices and space for creativity and exploration. Money can't buy happiness and true fulfilment.

The freedom to be ourselves is the greatest gift. –Oprah Winfrey

Baba, how come you remain so enthusiastic in life? Is there any divine power or force that made you so positive and energetic? My colleague and I become so exhausted at work that we get deprived of energy. Do you have any solutions?

Raghav, it seems that you are not working well to get your happy chemicals on track.

Happy chemicals? What does that mean, Baba?

For that, I will teach you some biology lessons today.

We all have some happy hormones that make us happy and energetic in life. In today's stressful lifestyle, most of the young men and women lack proper secretion of happy hormones. Humans are getting, day by day, far from nature, sunlight, plants, proper oxygen, pollution-driven environment, busy lifestyle, gadgets, intake of processed foods, and lack of proper nutritional foods. All these give rise to a decrease in the secretion of happy hormones in our body.

Our body secretes various hormones, like

1. Serotonin

2. Dopamine

3. Oxytocin, and

4. Endorphins

1. Serotonin – it is a chemical that carries messages between nerve cells in the brain and throughout your body. It helps in regulating your mood, sleep, digestion, sexual desires, and optimism. Serotonin levels are reduced when you are depressed.

2. Dopamine – it's a neurotransmitter, involved in movements, memory, pleasurable feelings, learning, mood, and it plays a small role in the fight or flight syndrome, the body's response in real stressful situations such as needing to escape danger. It is also called the "feel-good hormone." It gives a sense of pleasure; it provides motivation to do something. Junk food, pizza, burgers, and sugar are so addictive that they trigger the release of a large amount of dopamine in the body, making you feel happy and wanting to repeat that experience. If you have enough dopamine, you will feel happy and motivated.

3. Endorphins are the type of hormones that relieve pain and stress. The term endorphins come from the words "endogenous," meaning from the body, and "morphine," an opioid pain reliever. They reduce pain and discomfort, improve mood, and boost self-esteem. Our body releases them during pleasurable activities such as sex and exercise. They also promote memory and cognitive health and support a healthy immune system. Endorphins increase the feeling of well-being.

4. Oxytocin – it's also called the love hormone. Our body also produces oxytocin when we are excited by our sexual partner and when we fall in love. It plays an important role in many human behaviours and social interactions,

such as romantic attachment, parent-infant bonding, love, trust, and sexual arousal. It is a natural hormone that stimulates uterine contractions during childbirth and lactation after childbirth.

Baba, it means all these happy hormones are best friends of an individual.

Yes, Raghav, but everything is good within certain limits.

Now, Baba, please tell me how to improve the levels of all these happy hormones in the body.

It's very simple; we just have to live a healthy lifestyle to regulate the proper functioning of these happy hormones. You just have to sleep for at least 7-8 hours every day, take some morning sunlight, do some physical exercise every day, add enough green vegetables in your diet, and subtract sugar. Play with your children, hold hands with your partner, have a massage with some essential oils, walk in nature, spend some time in gardening, meditate for some time every day. If you follow all these rituals every day, you will become stress-free, and it will safeguard you from major lifestyle disorders.

16

FEAR OF DISEASE

"Fear of disease killed more men than the disease itself."

– Mahatma Gandhi

Baba, for the last 6 months, sometimes I feel pain in my stomach and sometimes in my right jaw below my ears. I have been suffering from constant anxiety about this. What if some life-threatening disease or cancer occurs to me in the near future? Who will take care of my family and my son? Sometimes at night, I don't get sleep thinking about it.

So, Raghav, what do you do at that time in the night?

Baba, I just Google about the symptoms and imagined the potential severity of the disease.

Oh Raghav, have you consulted about that to any medical practitioner? Yes, Baba, I have consulted about it many times to many practitioners, have gone through investigations also, but no abnormality detected. Fearing I have made term insurance of a huge amount, so that if something happens to me, then my family will not suffer.

Raghav, I believe you are suffering from **Cyberchondria.**

What does that mean, Baba?

One of my friends, Rishi, was also having symptoms like you. He had seen his relative suffering from stomach cancer. After that, he started thinking that his stomach pain would cause him stomach cancer in the near future.

Cyberchondria refers to a mental disorder in which a person searches excessively for health care information online on the internet but instead of finding relief for their concerns, diagnoses themselves with some terrible disease, and then feels more anxious. So, from now onwards, you should label your condition of worry as cyberchondria and believe that you can come out of it with practice.

I believe that most mental illnesses stem from a lack of sleep and exercise. When your mind and body are deprived of sleep, various hormonal changes occur in your body. Additionally, when you don't give your body proper rest, neglect physical movement or exercise, and fail to maintain good blood circulation, it can lead to health issues. Furthermore, a lack of proper nutrition and an excessive intake of junk and processed food can gradually weaken your immune system.

So, I think for the relief of your mental state, you should start sleeping early, wake up early in the morning, do some physical exercises, and start eating enough nutrients. Sooner or later, you will find positive changes in your body and mind.

According to scientists, if you have a fear of any disease in your mind for a long time, then your mind is capable of producing symptoms of that disease in your body because our brain is so powerful that if it can heal any disease, then it can create any disease, so always try to feed your brain with positive thoughts; it will help you in the near future.

One more thing I have noticed from my own experience is that whenever you get stuck with some minor disease, just change your environment for some days, move out to some new destinations, change your air, and water. You will see most of your minor illnesses will vanish.

So Raghav, just start with these things:

1. Sleep early and wake up early, sleep for around 8hours.
2. Do some physical exercises, yoga, meditation, and deep breathing exercises
3. Take proper nutrition.
4. Go for digital detox and take break from technology and consider for cognitive behavioural therapy or NLP from a therapist

Soon you will notice that most of your mental ailments and worrying habits will fade away with time.

17

BABA'S DAILY MORNING ROUTINE

"You'll never change your life until you change something you do daily. The secret to your success is found in your daily routine."

– John C. Maxwell

Baba, please tell me about your morning routine. I want to know how you start your day.

See Raghav, my morning routine starts a day before. I usually sleep between 9 to 10 pm. I am a strong believer in early to bed and early to rise. Studies on **circadian rhythms** reveal that sleeping between 9:00 pm and 12:00 am can yield enhanced sleep quality. This 3-hour window is considered a 'sleep multiplier', providing restorative sleep equivalent to 9 hours. This phenomenon is attributed to the body's natural production of melatonin and other sleep-regulating hormones during this period. Then, sleeping from 12 am to 3am yields approximately 2 hours of effective sleep, despite the 3-hour duration. This reduced sleep efficiency is attributed to the body's natural dip in melatonin levels and increased cortisol production during this period. Then, sleeping between 3 am and 7 am, despite the 4-hour duration, the body only receives approximately 1.5 hours of deep restorative sleep. This discrepancy is attributed to the body's natural cortisol increase and preparation for waking during this period.

So when I sleep at 9 pm and wake up between 5-6 am in the morning, this way I take around 12-13 hours of sleep.

Then after waking up, I make my bed as the first thing in the morning. I drink a big glass of warm water; sometimes I add lemon to it, sometimes triphla powder (an ayurvedic herbal rasayana formula consisting of 1:2:3 parts of 3 herbs i.e., Haritaki: Bibhitaki: Amalaki. It's high in vitamin C, which supports the immune system and also promotes digestion); sometimes moringa powder (obtained from the drumstick tree, a good source of B vitamins). Then, after answering nature's call, I move to nature, give water to plants in my garden and to the bird water feeder pot. Then I take 15mins of morning sunlight, it helps in the production of Vitamin D, essential for bone health and immune functions. Beyond powering solar cells to produce electricity, sunlight offers numerous benefits to human body. After that, I go to my nearby park for some exercise and a walk, and I perform around 21 surya namaskar along with some yoga postures. Then, I do some breathing exercises. I inhale through my nose and exhale through my mouth slowly 15 to 20 times, and then I do some meditation for 15-20 minutes.

Then I read a few pages of some good books, both fiction and non-fiction. I like to read. Then around 7, I usually take a bath, and after taking a bath, I always clean my bathroom myself. I feel it's very important to clean your bathroom. In Japanese customs, they emphasise on cleaning your bathroom to cleanse your karmas. Then I offer water to the sun from my small copper jar. It increases a sense of discipline. In our culture, surya prayer bestows us the power to get rid of troubles and showers confidence and prosperity.

Then I make my healthy breakfast and start my routine. For the first 3 hours of the day, I give time to my body, mind, and soul, and it rejuvenates me throughout the day.

18

SIX PILLARS OF HOLLISTC LIVING

Baba, this is the last question I ask you today before leaving for Dubai tomorrow. What is the secret of having a wonderful and fulfilled life?

Raghav I will tell you not one, not 2, but 6 pointers that, if you follow, you will have a satisfied and fulfilled life.

1. **Health**

"Health is not valued until sickness comes,"

– Thomas Fuller.

If God comes and asks you, "Why should I give you good health and a disease-free, healthy life?" Do you have any answer for that?

Having good health should be your first and foremost priority in life because if you don't have good health, you won't be able to enjoy your life in the future. We all neglect this concept in our life, and after a certain age, we realise that we should have given some time for our health in our young life to maintain it. When we suffer from any disease, only at that time we do realise the importance of good health, and believe me, nothing comes free of charge in life. We have to pay for having good health. We need to give time for maintaining our health. Physical and mental healths both are important. Physical health can't be good without mental health and vice versa. The previous generation did a lot of physical work which this generation does not do.

While running after wealth, we always forget to give time to our health, and after a certain age, we regret it. A wealthy man always searches for health, and a healthy man always searches for wealth.

Without good health, you cannot become good parents or good life partners. The luckiest children are those whose parents are fit and healthy, without any disease, because your illness can sometimes burden your children and the whole family. Not only you, but your spouse and children also suffer from your illness. I have seen entire families suffer due to a major health issue affecting an elderly family member. It also impacts the family's financial stability. Consequently, they may have to give up their hobbies and passions due to a severe illness or the premature death of a parent. Therefore, never take your health for granted.

If you do not take your health issues seriously, it will result in high medical bills and unforeseen expenses in the future, resulting in a low bank balance.

So, always give time to maintain your health. It will provide you maximum returns and save you a lot of money in the future.

Spend at least one hour in the morning doing any physical activity, such as gym, yoga, zumba, aerobics, running, cycling, jogging, etc., that takes out sweat from your body and also improves blood circulation. Just one hour out of 24 hrs, and you will see tremendous changes in your body and mind. Take proper nutrition and avoid junk and processed food; avoid excessive sugar and salt. Add enough protein and vitamins in your diet, eat less and digest more, take enough good bacteria present in curd, and have your last meal before 8.00 pm at night.

And for mental health, start sitting with closed eyes for 10 mins a day for meditation, and gradually take it to 30 minutes. Prefer doing it on an empty stomach. Morning or evening, anytime which suits you. It will reduce your stress levels, and you will have a sound sleep, which will regulate the proper functioning of your hormones. Anxiety, depression, and stress are very much common these days. The number of suicide cases are increasing every year due to depression. For that, you need to pay attention to your body for a healthy, disease-free living.

2. Financial Literacy

"Financial literacy gives you the opportunity to be confident and empowered to live the quality of life you have worked for."

– Erin Beable.

Baba, how come you never felt deprived of money? What were your financial plans when you were young? Please tell me about your financial journey of making money.

Raghav I always believes that any fool can make money, but it needs financial education to manage and multiply it. I have seen people receiving millions from their ancestral property or making millions by winning lottery tickets, but after some time, due to a lack of financial education, they lost most of their wealth and went back to the same position where they started.

I always believed the power of compounding as the eighth wonder of the world. You need to read books and articles by Warren Buffet and Robert Kiyosaki.

Whenever you start earning, at any age, may be 20-24, you should develop a habit of investing at least 10% of your income. Of course, health insurance and term insurance must be your first priority while investing, and an emergency fund of 6 months' income should be kept aside in a savings bank account or fixed deposit.

There are many assets you can invest in, like equity, fixed deposits, commodities like gold and silver, real estate, bonds, and government provident funds which give guaranteed returns.

All investment options have their pros and cons. The more the risk more is the returns; the less the risk, the less the returns.

According to Warren Buffett, "Never keep all your eggs in the same basket." That means you should always diversify your investment portfolio.

If you are married and have a family to take care of, I will advise you that the first and foremost thing you should take is term insurance. I have seen many families and the ladies of the family suffering poorly and working very hard for the survival of the family after the death of their husband.

Children have to compromise on their studies after the death of their father at an early age just because their father didn't manage to get appropriate term insurance. If you love your family, term insurance is a must. Life is always uncertain.

Then there come health insurance. With time, the immunity of coming generations will diminish. Medical inflation is rising day by day, and you will lose a major portion of your wealth if you don't have medical insurance. I have seen people losing their properties and bank balance during pandemic seasons. You need to pay to the hospitals in times of any health adversity; you have no choices then. I have seen people taking loans to pay their hospital bills. Medical insurance is the need of the hour. And always say thanks to God the year you don't use your medical insurance policy.

Then there comes equity. If you have confidence in the growth of your country's economy, the best thing to invest in is equity. It is said that if you keep investing 10,000rs per month and continue it for 20 years, you can easily build a corpus of around 1 crore at a rate of 12 percent compound annual growth rate at the end of 20 years. This includes investing directly in the stock market or investing through mutual funds and exchange-traded funds. It depends on your risk profile. Stocks have higher risks but returns are also higher. Mutual funds have lower risks but returns are also less compared to stocks. Stocks are of large companies as well as small companies. Large company stocks are less risky than small company stocks. But investing is equity is market linked, returns are not guaranteed.

Then there comes commodity. It includes investing mainly gold and silver. The value of gold and silver will increase with time. The value of 10gms of gold was 4400rs in 2000, but in 2024, it's equivalent to 75,000 Rs. After 20 years, if it continues to grow at the same rate of 12.5%, the value of 10gm of gold would be around 7 lac and 90 thousand rupees. That's the power of compounding. Both gold and silver have limited availability in the world.

Then there comes various govt-supported guaranteed plans. They are the safest with minimal returns, and many of them give tax benefits. Public Provident Fund, National Pension System, National Savings Certificate, Kisan Vikas Patra, fixed deposits, Sukanya Samriddhi, etc. They have lock-in periods and are usually available at around 6 to 7 percent interest rates.

Then there comes real estate. In India, most of the people are fond of real estate properties. People buy land and flats; with time, the value of land rises. It is one of the safest investments. However, they have very low liquidity; selling real estate takes time. You need huge money to buy it. There may also be a threat of capture by mafias. Many people like to have rental income through real estate investments. Not all real estate properties' values increase at the same rate over time.

Both equity and gold have grown at the rate of around 12% per annum for the last 20 years. So, if you are 25 years old and have started investing, I would advise you to invest in both equity and gold. Undoubtedly, you need to own a house, and for that, you have to invest in real estate, but it requires a substantial capital. I consider a house a liability, not an asset.

When you get your salary in the first week of the month, first try to invest your decided amount and then utilise the rest of the amount. People just do the opposite; they first utilise the money on needs and desires and invest the remaining corpus.

As Warren Buffett said, don't keep all of your eggs in the same basket, it's very essential to diversify your portfolio. And if you don't know how to manage your money, you can always hire a financial adviser, since he is an expert in that field. Likewise, a doctor is an expert in medicine, and an architect is an expert in his field.

It's your hard-earned money; never rely blindly on investment ideas given by any layman or relative person. You should do your research before investing your money. I have seen people losing their entire retirement corpus due to investing their entire corpus in fake companies, by taking advice from wrong persons. It is advisable to always diversify your corpus.

The power of compounding works wonders when you start investing as early as possible.

When your income is very low in the initial years, I will advise you to start investing in yourself. Read good books, improve your skills; communication skills should be learned. All these learning will help you dramatically enhance your income in the long run. It's always said that if you learn more, you will earn more. You should always have a learner's mindset because knowledge has no limits. The more you learn, the more you realise there is much more to learn. There is a saying: never try to become a master; always try to become a good student. It will help you achieve more in life.

One more piece of advice I will give you is to never rely on your children for your retirement. I have seen people of my age complaining about their children, not sending them a bit of their income, never visiting them to serve their needs, never taking time for the treatment of their illness. I always ask them, "Have you produced children or have you made any investment policy?" Don't expect a return on investments from your children. They have their own life; they are busy solving their own problems. Never depend on children for help in old age. For that, you have to plan for your retirement goals so that in your old age, you need not ask for any materialistic help from your children. I always believe that kids should be treated like birds; when they grow up, they will fly in the sky to find their own world and life. You should not expect anything from your kids. In fact, you should teach them about financial education and the difference between assets and liabilities at a very young age.

Assets are the things you buy that will bring money into your pocket and that will grow with time, like gold, shares, or a piece of land. You will have price appreciation in the future.

Liabilities are the things that you buy that won't bring money into your pocket, like mobile phones, vehicles, expensive watches, etc.

You should always have a balance between your assets and liabilities. If you invest only in assets, then you won't enjoy life, and if you buy only liabilities, then you won't become rich with time.

One more thing I will tell you is to always make a nominee in your investments. There are many who forget to nominate their investments, and when they die, their family members really don't know about their investments.

One habit I always had is that I always write my expenses, so in this way; I always have a check on where my money is getting utilised. Whenever you spend money, even a single coin, you should have a habit of writing it down. So, at the end of the month, you can track your expenses. There is nothing wrong with spending money, but you should know where you are spending it. Suppose you have a habit of smoking, drinking alcohol, and partying with friends. If you write it down and evaluate it at the end of the month, then only you will come to know that you are spending a major portion of your income on addiction and vanity, and you may take action to stop it. Then your mind will tell you to have control over your expenses for the next month.

Also there is a financial rule of 50: 30: 20. It will give you a sense of security and help you achieve future goals. This rule states that you should spend 50% of your monthly income on necessities like food, transportation, medical and electricity bills, and other household items essential for your survival. Allocate 30% towards your desires, meaning things that are not necessary but that your heart desires, such as dining in a hotel, going to the cinema, buying luxury items, clothes, going on vacations, buying cars, or gym memberships. The remaining 20% should be dedicated to financial goals, including savings that are invested to yield returns in the future for your retirement, buying a house, and clearing debts and loans.

You should always make a goal of how much corpus you need to build in what span of time. You need to be specific in terms of this number, and the goals must be big; there is no excitement in mediocrity.

There was a study conducted at Howard University in 1979, in which at the time of convocation students were asked about the goal of their life. 84% of students were not able to clearly define their goal, 13% of students had a goal in their mind, and the remaining 3% had written their goal on a paper kept with them.

After 10 years, the university surveyed again about their students, and they found that 13% of the students who had their goal in mind were earning more than 84% of the students who lacked making goals, and the remaining 3% who had written their goal on a piece of paper and kept it with them were earning more than the 13% of students who kept the goal in their mind. This study clearly proved that if you have a written goal, the chances are great that you would most likely achieve it.

When Bill Gates and Warren Buffet, the 2 biggest billionaires, were asked in an interview what the most important thing is to achieve success in life?

They both had the same answer, which is to focus on your goal.

I always believe in self-development, or you can say that you need to upgrade yourself. In whatever field you are, if you are not upgrading, it means you are degrading. You need to develop skills, whether it's communication skills, public speaking skills, sales skills, product development skills; there are numerous skills that can take you to new heights in this competitive world. You will gain the skills only when you focus on self-development. Successful people have this quality of utilising their maximum time in learning new skills. You need to connect with people who are upgrading themselves. The day you stop learning, I believe your progress will be over. Attend various seminars and workshops, both online and offline; they will all take you to new heights in life.

In order to be rich and successful, you should always try to add value to the life of others, and then money will be a by-product of that value. You should be a good problem solver; you should try to make the life of people around you much easier. A lawyer solves the problems of their clients; in this way, he adds value to their clients. A doctor adds value to his patients and earns from them. A teacher adds value to his students and earns accordingly. When you solve a small problem, you will earn a small amount; the bigger the problem you solve, the more you will earn.

3. Relationships

"All relationships have one law. Never make the one you love feel alone, especially when you are there."

– Anonymous

One should know the importance of making, managing, and polishing relations. We humans need people to have a bond with, to laugh with, and to tell our stories. There are some relations who are god-gifted and some we make; both are important to maintain. God-gifted relations are our parents, siblings, uncles, cousins, etc., and man-made relations are friends, colleagues, and people at the workplace, servants, and others.

After a certain age, nearly 20, people tend to lose interest in familial relations. Since they lack time to maintain it, they enjoy spending more time with friends. They may have other career priorities at this age, thereby tending to lose bonds with cousins and siblings with whom they used to play during childhood. After some point, we tend to realise the importance of these relations when we need to share our success and failure stories with them.

In order to maintain healthy relations with people, we need to work on developing these qualities:

a. Communication - regular conversations are the key point to start and maintain any relationship. The moment we neglect the importance of conversations, we begin to lose our relationships.

b. Be trustworthy. you should always try not to break the trust of people around you. When people lose trust in you, your profile gets distorted in their mind.

c. Listen - when you pay attention to people's opinions, they feel that you are taking interest in them. This gives a boost to make new relations and maintain old relations.

d. Time - you need to give time to people in order to maintain your relationships. Many people lose their relationships when they fail to give quality time to people around them. You can engage in shared activities so you can create good memories. Many people who prefer to earn more money and prioritise work and money over relationships tend to lose their relations, so be prepared to lose some bucks if you want to maintain healthy relationships.

e. Forgiveness - let go of grudges and work towards resolution. Everyone has their own perspective, and you should accept this difference in opinion. Try to apologise when you make any mistake; everyone makes mistakes, but he who apologises can save relationships. A little bit of compromise is acceptable in relationships.

f. Never let people feel unheard or ignored - In today's world of technology and advancement, many a time you get so busy with your smartphone that you really don't care whether the person sitting beside you wants to spend time with you. Always try to put your smartphone aside when someone is speaking.

4. Spirituality

"You do not need to work to become spiritual. You are spiritual; you need only to remember that fact. Spirit is within you. God is within you."

– Julia Cameron.

It is a very broad concept to understand. Many religions have their own different opinions on spirituality. But to make it easier to understand, I will explain the meaning of spirituality to you in just one line - **Spirituality is a way to create Harmony within Yourself.**

Some people say that being religious means being spiritual, but in some sense, it's true. While some people define spirituality by being more focused on your work that is also true in some sense.

What I feel is it's more or less being opposite to violence, but some people might use spiritual beliefs to justify their violent actions. On the other hand, violent behaviour might stem from pain and trauma, which can be addressed through spiritual growth and support.

Spirituality lays emphasis on connecting yourself to something greater, a sense of belonging to a larger universe, nature, or higher power. When you become religious, some part of your soul converts to spirituality, since when you become religious, you embrace values, beliefs, principles, ethics, and convictions, and that is being spiritual.

Being religious cultivates practicing kindness and adopting non-violence, and it's one way to be spiritual.

By practicing yoga and meditation, some part of your soul becomes spiritual. When you practice yoga and meditation, you cultivate awareness, mindfulness, and living in the present moment.

Having a purposeful life makes you spiritual. It implies that you are brought here in this world for a purpose to solve problems of the world, both directly and indirectly, and your objective should be to make this world a better place to live. So, when you become dedicated and focus more on your work, you become spiritual.

Having a feeling of gratitude, by appreciating the beauty and blessings in your life, makes you spiritual.

I know one of my friend's daughters, Dr. Prisha, a neurologist, advocates practicing spirituality to create a balance between body, mind, and soul. Having a spiritual mind can positively accept the jerks and setbacks in life.

In essence, spirituality and harmony are intertwined aspects of human experience. Spirituality can lead to greater harmony, and harmony supports spiritual growth.

5. Contributions

"Life is not accumulation; it is about contribution."

– Stephen Covey.

The prime objective of mankind should be to contribute, whether to humanity, welfare of animals, the environment, or nature. It gives a message to the universe that your existence is important for nature, and in return, the universe helps you in numerous ways for your survival. You will notice that each and every one is contributing in some way or other. A doctor contributes by curing, a lawyer contributes by fighting for justice, a teacher contributes by providing knowledge and skills, a driver contributes by transporting passengers or cargo. He who doesn't care to contribute, the universe doesn't pay him any reward.

There are various ways of contributions, like by donating money for the survival of the poor and needy, donating money for the maintenance of religious places, by donating food, by giving your time serving as volunteers, by donating blood or organs before or after death, by educating, or by sponsoring education. In Hinduism and Jainism, it's a culture to serve cows and dogs by offering their first bread of the day. You can also contribute to the living and survival of saints.

Some people contribute just for uploading pictures on social media to improve their social status, while some people like to contribute without disclosing their name. I don't feel anything wrong in both cases.

Contribution to religious places is also important because it requires maintenance charges such as cleanliness, electricity bills, salaries for pujaris, and construction and maintenance of dharamshalas.

Whenever you contribute, try to do it wholeheartedly, not just for the sake of it or forcefully and never ever expect anything in return.

I have seen some people contribute 5 percent of their income, some 10 percent, and some even 90 percent. It's up to you what you are capable of.

There are 5 psychological benefits of contributing to society or the universe.

1. It increases your sense of purpose for living. It increases your worth in your eyes.

2. It reduces the symptoms of depression, anxiety, and stress. When you contribute, you feel connected to the universe.

3. It improves your self-esteem. It has a positive impact on your mental health.

4. Inner peace and satisfaction. You feel content and fulfilled.

5. It is one of the finest ways to improve your spiritual growth.

Finding ways to give back to nature can bring you joy and fulfilment. There was someone who thought of contributing to humanity by inventing anaesthesia and painkiller medicines. Can you imagine your life where you undergo a tooth extraction without anaesthesia?

Never delay contribution by thinking that when I will cross a certain age or when I will reach a certain stage in life, then I will start contributing. Who knows when you will leave this world, so start contributing now in whichever way you like.

6. Learning

"Develop a passion for learning. If you do, you will never cease to grow."

– Anthony J. D'Angelo.

Learning is a lifelong process by which we acquire knowledge, skills, attitude, new understanding, and values. A person who doesn't have a learning mindset is like a ship sailing on water just with the flow of winds without having any direction. Minds that have an attitude of learning always remain young despite age. Learning new skills expands your neural connections in the brain, which helps to prevent age-related mental disorders like dementia.

But you need to spend something for learning, whether it's time, money, energy, or effort. Learning can be acquired with the help of books, mentors, workshops, courses, YouTube, and other online platforms. Never hesitate to spend money on learning, since learning increases your earning capacity.

Any sort of learning or skill enhancement programme is useful for your growth, whether its communication skills, art and crafts, painting, cooking, or any sports, etc.

Those who start learning get to know that they know very little. Learning increases the hunger to know more and more about any subject.

Many a time, after school days, we leave the habit of reading books. Many great thinkers and billionaires share a common habit of reading books.

Reading good books has numerous benefits like vocabulary building, expanded knowledge, communication skill improvement, improved memory and concentration, reduced stress and anxiety, enhanced focus and creativity with imagination, enhanced curiosity, emotional and mental well-being, and can help to prevent cognitive decline and age-related mind disorders.

It is said that you become what goes into your mind. If you read good books, goodness comes to you.

You may learn something new with books. The book can be in your field or any personal growth non-fiction self-help book. You can learn through mentors by attending workshops. You should always try to upgrade yourself, since if you are not upgrading, you are downgrading. Even your Smartphone requests you to update it in a few months.

Learning anything new is a great way to channelize your negative emotions or energy when you are in deep sorrow. Learning new things at that time is a must for those who are in deep grief due to a failure or loss of any loved one. It helps you to come out of your anxiety and depression.

I have never seen any learner who has a negative mindset. Learners always have a positive mentality and approach towards life. They believe in themselves and are always ready to take on new challenges in life. If you reach a certain level in your career and you feel that your growth is stagnant now, then make sure you are not left with a learning attitude. After reaching a certain level in a profession, we start thinking that we know everything, and there is nothing left to learn. That is the point where your growth comes to an end. Continuous upgrading is necessary for continuous growth.

Learning surely increases your earning capacity. You are what you know. Learning just requires your time and efforts, and sometimes money; you just need to limit your time for instant gratification of scrolling reels. I have read somewhere that learning a new language has a profound positive impact on the neural plasticity of your brain.

You should try to associate yourself with a company of learners or make friends with learning mindsets. It is always believed that learning is contagious. If you spend time with a learner, you immerse yourself in the process of learning skills. If you see your friend reading a book, there are chances that you will also cultivate this habit.

So always try to be surrounded by ambitious learners who want to achieve something big in life.

Thank you so much, Baba, for providing me with such great knowledge of life. I promise you that tomorrow, after returning to Dubai, I will share all these 16 masterstroke ideas to elevate life with people out there in the world.

CLOSING CEREMONY

After 2 hours of holding the microphone and speaking continuously, Raghav sipped a glass of water.

Memories of Baba's gentle smile and twinkling eyes flooded my mind, now tinged with a hint of sadness. I recalled the way his eyes sparkled while sharing tales of adventure, his voice filled with a deep wisdom that commanded attention. My heart ached, remembering the day he left us, his passing leaving a gaping hole in our lives. Yet even in death, his legacy lived on, a testament to the love, wisdom, and memories he shared with me. As I sat in the silence, surrounded by the echoes of his presence, I knew that his memory would continue to inspire and guide me, a bittersweet reminder of the precious time we had together.

As the award ceremony drew to a close, the crowd began to disperse, and the room slowly emptied. The excitement and the glamour of the evening gave way to a sense of closure and farewell. Guests exchanged warm smiles, hugs, and handshakes. As the lights dimmed, the stagehands began to disassemble the set, and the orchestra packed up their instruments. The once-filled auditorium grew quiet. Outside, the cool night air greeted the departing guests, refreshing contrasts to the warmth and energy of the ceremony. Some hailed taxis, while others made their way to their cars parked in the nearby lot.

The guests carried with them memories of a night to remember.

ABOUT THE AUTHOR

Dr. Ravi Surana is a distinguished dentist renowned for his exceptional service to the community of Sirohi district, Rajasthan, India since 2011. His passion for dentistry is truly remarkable, setting a high standard for quality care. Through his steady commitment to excellence, he has significantly raised the bar for oral healthcare in his region. Recently, he has been elected as secretary of the Indian Dental Association of the district branch. Although he has received more than 30 awards and certificates by undergoing various workshops both offline and online across the globe, he spends a significant amount of time reading books and has an insatiable appetite for knowledge about mindset, psychology, finances, spirituality, and travel. He is passionate about exploring new ideas, perspectives, and worlds through reading. He is very fond of travelling. He likes to keep exploring, keep discovering, and keep pushing boundaries.

INSPIRING YOU TO WRITE

Want to be remembered long after you're gone? Write a book! It's a timeless legacy that will continue to inspire and educate.

Don't think you can? I believed in myself, and so can you.

Start writing and let your words live on.

Movies cost millions to make, but sometimes they flop. You haven't spent millions to write a book. The worst case scenario is your book might flop, but that's not the end of the world. At least 4 out of 100 people will appreciate your work.

By writing a book you are taking a calculated risk to pursue your creativity. You are investing time and effort into your passion. You are not stressing about your book's success or failure. You are simply following your dream.

Keep writing and working towards your goal. Your book will find its audience.

Dr. Ravi Surana

ravisurana999@gmail.com

CONCLUSIONS

Dear friend.

Congratulations on completing "The Rising Mindset"! Our journey together has just begun.

I hope you enjoyed this book as much as I enjoyed writing it; however, reading alone is not enough. To transform your relationships, influence others, and achieve success, you must apply these principles.

Knowledge is potential power but application is the real power, so start small today;

1. Choose your favourite strategies.
2. Practice them daily.
3. Watch small changes compound into significant growth.

Become a doer, it's worth it.

If this book has positively impacted your life or you have suggestions, please share

Ravisurana999@gmail.com

Wishing you an excellent future filled with happiness, health, wealth and success.

Best Regards,

Dr. Ravi Surana

ANOTHER PERSPECTIVE ON SUCCESS

On earth we measure success by reaching financial stability or professional achievement but who knows on some other planet success is measured by achieving peace of mind, better relationships or better health.

We need to rethink our values and priorities and consider alternative definition of success and strive for balance and stress free holistic well- being.

What if success is measured by the positive impact on environment?

How would society change if empathy and compassion are key success metrics?

Imagine a world where lifelong learning and personal growth are ultimate goals in life.

What if success is defined by the number of meaningful connections and relationships?

Think about it.

Let's make this world a better place to live.